ALSO BY GARY MOREAU

NON-FICTION

Understanding China: There is Reason for the Difference

Understanding Business: The Logic of Balance

Understanding Life: Context is Everything

FICTION

Now You Are Lisa

By Avam Hale (an early pen name)

The Message?

The Bomb Shelter

We, Ourselves, and Us

We, Ourselves, and Us

CREATING A MORE JUST AND
PROSPEROUS AMERICA

• • •

Gary Moreau

© 2018 Gary Moreau
All rights reserved.

ISBN: 1983680273
ISBN-13: 9781983680274

For my daughters, Leah and Ava;

May we leave you and yours a better world.

Contents

Dedication vii

Introduction 1
Chapter 1   Individualism 9
Chapter 2   Change 21

Part I Economic 31
Chapter 3   Division of Labor 33
Chapter 4   Corporate Personhood 41
Chapter 5   Corporate Ownership 50
Chapter 6   Our Digital World 60

Part II Social 71
Chapter 7   Wages 73
Chapter 8   Media 85
Chapter 9   Education 100
Chapter 10   Private Property 111

Part III Political 121
Chapter 11   Rule of Law 123

Chapter 12 Unintended Consequences.................... 132
Chapter 13 Democratic Elections....................... 144
Chapter 14 Centralization............................. 156

Moving Forward.. 169
Conclusion 171
From the Author....................................... 181
About the Author 183

Introduction

• • •

We the people...

—Preamble to the US Constitution

The premise of this book is pretty simple. Or at least straightforward. It is that the economic, political, and social systems and institutions that collectively define the United States and shape the lives of Americans have become both more complex and more integrated over time. We have, as a result, surpassed the tipping point at which the supremacy of the individual, the "I" in all our freedoms and liberties, threatens the hope and vitality that gave life and purpose to American exceptionalism and the American Century.

Doubling down on the supremacy of "I" by either dismantling government or enshrining new individual liberties in regulatory protection, the apparent strategies of conservative Republicans and liberal Democrats aren't going to help. The former turns back the clock to a time and place that no longer exists. The latter anticipates a social, economic, and political context that is not yet in place and will not uphold the commitment.

Continuing down the current path with renewed vigor and enthusiasm, however, won't work either. A path only exists in context (e.g., among the trees of a forest, amid the grass of a meadow, or along the cliffs of a mountain), and the historical context that helped to define, and was in turn shaped by, our current path doesn't align with the context of our current reality.

Driven largely by rapid advancements in technology that have completely altered how we live, work, learn, and play, the traditional path of individual liberties and freedoms has lost both its relevance and effectiveness. In the context of twenty-first century America, it is a path suspended in air, without the substance and foundation to support our weight. Passionately divided, we stand dazed, confused, and often bewildered at the crossroads of our traditional values and the systems they shaped, and a future world defined by machine learning and artificial intelligence, an increasingly fragile ecosystem, and a burgeoning population searching for individual identity in the context of our mutual dependence and hunger for peace and unity.

Of course we want to move forward. We all want the economy to grow. We all want to protect our shared environment. We all want sustainable and better wages for our labor. We all want to prepare our children for the future. We all want the security of accessible and affordable health care. There are no red states and blue states when it comes to defining the American dream.

Neither the red nor the blue strategies we are collectively pursuing, however, moves us in that direction. Both paths offer outdated solutions to old problems defined within an obsolete context. Neither will lead us forward. We need a new path that fits securely in the reality of our current context.

The liberal democracy, as we've known it, cannot survive. Not because it is inherently flawed or unattractive, but because it is irrelevant to the context of the times. It no longer fits.

What will emerge, and has already emerged, whether blue or red, is a one-dimensional autocracy that will, by definition, alienate large blocks of the population in pursuit of solutions that no longer reflect the real problems at hand. We all want to make America great again. But we can't move forward by retracing the path of rugged individualism that brought us here. That path will not take us back to where we were because that place no longer exists.

We need a new path forward that recognizes and leverages current reality for our collective betterment. We need a new path that builds on the achievements of liberal democracy while adapting to current reality so that our momentum can carry us forward to an even more prosperous, inclusive, and peaceful future where technology and learning are embraced, where we may individually and collectively thrive, and where "*we* the people" can attain the original goals of "life, liberty, and the pursuit of happiness."

It is possible. And it doesn't require armed revolution or political upheaval. It can be achieved incrementally and at a pace that we find acceptable. We don't need to blow up the trail. We need only to redefine the trail markers.

Specifically, we need to replace the American "I" with the collective "We." We need only adapt to the new context of a global, integrated, technologically empowered world in which justice is ensured and opportunity is accelerated through transparent policies and institutions that promote the collective good.

Collectivism, of course, has existed in the United States since its founding in the form of utopian communities, some of which still exist today. Following the principles of common property and equality in all things, the Shakers attracted roughly six thousand members, living in twenty communities, by the 1830s. British socialist Robert Owen, pursuing not religious purity but social perfection, founded New Harmony, Indiana, in 1825, although it lasted only two years before collapsing financially. Brook Farm, established in West Roxbury, Massachusetts, in 1841, adhered to the transcendental beliefs of the great thinkers of the era and counted Ralph Waldo Emerson, Nathaniel Hawthorne, and Henry David Thoreau among its regular visitors.

John Humphrey Noyes and his followers formed the Oneida Community on the banks of the creek of the same name in upstate New York in 1848. The community, hugely successful in economic terms, disbanded in 1880 but put all its common assets into a joint stock company, ultimately called Oneida Ltd., which still markets the community's famous silverware today. Of no relation to any original community member, I would find my first job there, under the leadership of John Humphrey's grandson Pierrepont ("Pete") T. Noyes and would ultimately become the company's president in the course of my eighteen-year career there. The original community experimented with group marriage and communal child rearing, but was perhaps best known for its inventive and egalitarian culture, which greatly influenced the corporate culture more than a century later, during my own tenure there.

The popularity of utopian communities peaked in the mid-nineteenth century, but some remain active today. Twin Oaks, in Virginia, was founded in 1967, and The Farm, in Lewis County, Tennessee, was founded in 1971 and operates today as a model for sustainable living. Steve Jobs, the larger-than-life guiding spirit of Apple, worked in an apple orchard belonging to a commune called All One Farm near McMinnville, Oregon. It was founded by Reed College schoolmate Robert Friedland, and it was this orchard that ultimately inspired the name Jobs gave his company.

When Americans think of collectivist states, however, they normally think of socialism and communism. Karl Marx and Friedrich

Engels wrote the *Communist Manifesto* in 1848, introducing the expression "scientific socialism," which would influence politics across Europe and around the world to this day.

The Socialist Party of America was formed in 1901 and enjoyed early support from socialist reformers, farmers, and trade unionists. It elected two US representatives and more than one hundred mayors. Its presidential candidate in 1912 and 1920, Eugene V. Debs, won over nine hundred thousand votes in each of his campaigns. Although that sounds like a small number today, America was a lot smaller then, and the right to vote was enjoyed by only a portion of the white male population.

The Socialist Party suffered notable defections over its opposition to World War I and was fractured over the question of how to treat the October Revolution in Russia in 1917. The Communist Party USA grew out of the rift and went on to be a highly influential force in various struggles for democratic rights, particularly relating to the budding labor movement. Until, of course, the Cold War and McCarthyism crippled the party's support. By the end of the era, membership was down to a few thousand, and many of those were rumored to be informants for J. Edgar Hoover's FBI.

The Soviet Union was the most famous example of a modern communist state, although much of the tyranny Americans normally associate with the *gulag* state came from Vladimir Lenin and the Bolsheviks, who came to power in the second revolution of 1917 and formed the Union of Soviet Socialist Republics (USSR), under the control of the Communist Party, in 1922.

Marx and Engel, in fact, never really articulated what their socialist state might look like, limiting their characterization of Marxism to the paradigm of class struggle and oppression and the inevitability of a proletarian class revolution that would end capitalism and usher in a classless, stateless society based on the elimination of private property and the ideal: "From each according to his ability, to each according to his needs."

The most successful modern communist state has been China, although the Communist Party of China refers to its governance model as "socialism with Chinese characteristics." In reality, China operates a hybrid model that recognizes both common and private property rights and both central and decentralized economic planning. Suffice it to say that China today would be unrecognizable to either Marx or Engel as an example of what they had in mind.

At the same time, the United States itself does not operate a direct, popular democracy, nor does its economy meet the standard of free market capitalism that Adam Smith wrote about in *Wealth of Nations*. It, too, operates a hybrid system of representative democracy and government-guided markets.

Nearly all of the economic, political, and social governance models in existence today, in fact, are hybrid models to one degree or another. Virtually all, however, expound on the supremacy and importance of the individual. When American leaders talk about governance, they talk almost exclusively about individual rights and freedoms, the right to free speech and expression, the right to own guns, the right to religious freedom, and the right to personal happiness and well-being.

I take no exception with this individual-centric ideal. I embrace its conceptual foundation. But I fear greatly for the hypocrisy it represents. It is not the world we live in. In reality, we live in a tribal world in a constant state of war. The only individual we celebrate and protect is the self. We don't live in the "I" world; we live in the "ME" world. And there's a huge difference. The "I" world looks outward. The "ME" world looks only inward. The "I" world that created American exceptionalism is a world of individual opportunity. The

"ME" world, by contrast, is consumed with individual outcomes—I want, I deserve, it's mine.

The we-centric collectivism that I will describe in the pages of this book is more than a horse of a different color. It's not a horse. It is a collective being perfectly suited to its environment. It is a new form of collectivism that does not enslave or denigrate the individual, but celebrates our common humanity and embraces our individual creativity and drive toward the advancement of our collective well-being.

To clarify what I mean, let me borrow the analogy of the environment. At one time we considered the components of our global environment to be largely discrete and independent. We had a fertile prairie here, an ice cap there, and a rain forest somewhere far away. Scientists have discovered, however, that these are all part of a complex, integrated global ecosystem that requires a delicate balance between many discrete but integrated subsystems.

As governance systems, socialism and communism recognized the integration of the political, economic, and social spheres, but failed to appreciate that it is balance, not mere coordination, and certainly not wishful thinking, that drives ecological sustainability and health. It is balance itself, not its component forces, that creates both the desired opportunity and the desired outcome.

Doctors and medical researchers have discovered the same thing in terms of the human body. The modern discrete, organ-centric approach to medicine is quickly being replaced by holistic wellness that recognizes, promotes, and, when necessary, restores the balance of the body's biological, digestive, intellectual, and emotional systems. There are still occasions when we need to physically repair a component of the physical system, but the nature of these functional repairs are undertaken within a very different, more complete, and inclusive context of medicine and health.

What I am proposing, therefore, is no different than what the scientists of ecology and the doctors of medicine are already doing. I am merely applying the holistic, integrated model they developed to the arenas of political, economic, and social governance. Instead of treating each of these systems as discrete and independent, I am merely integrating them into one inclusive system of *we-centric collectivism*.

For clarity and brevity I will refer to this new integrated system as an ecosystem of governance. An ecosystem, as I use the term, is any system or network of interconnected elements that recognizes both the integration of its parts and the overall context within which they function. A human is an organism that lives in the context of an environment. Together they form an ecosystem.

The we-centric ecosystem is, in the end, neither individualistic nor collective. It is a system of relativity, not absolutes. Paradoxically, it will look a lot more like the "I" world of the young America than it will the "ME" world of America today. It is the "I"-centric model modified for the more crowded, more complex, and more integrated America we live in. You might think of it as "I" 2.0, a model of individuality built for the scale and complexity of the modern world.

Whatever we call it, its purpose and its operation are defined not by the rights and behavior of me, myself, and I, but by the *balance* achieved among we, ourselves, and us.

CHAPTER 1

Individualism

• • •

One for all, and all for one.

—Alexandre Dumas (1844), *The Three Musketeers*

Historical demographers estimate that the population of the world in 1800 was around one billion people. The current global population is roughly 7.3 billion people, and by most estimates, it will reach ten billion by the middle of the century.

That's the equivalent of adding more than one thousand cities the size of New York City in just two hundred and fifty years. Beyond the obvious strain that will put on the global environment, such extreme growth will overwhelm the institutions that define our society, our politics, and our economy.

But it gets worse. The problem is not that our institutions cannot keep up. The real tragedy will be the dystopian, repressive, and unjust world that the conventions we use to define and allocate power within these institutions will result in. Who will want to survive other than the handful of elite—probably white men, if nothing changes—who will be pulling the levers of oppression and self-enrichment?

The reality exposed by the #MeToo campaign, Black Lives Matter, and the various positions taken by pastry chefs and local government clerks in an effort to quash the rights of the LGBT community paint an irrefutable picture of a nation that has lost its way on the road to progress. This is not the American dream envisioned by the men and women who built this country, and it is not the dream I, now a sexagenarian, assumed we would pass on to our children.

This is a national nightmare in which the top 1 percent of Americans own 40 percent of the wealth and the bottom 90 percent are responsible for almost three-fourths of all debt; women hold only 20 percent of the seats in the US Congress, while women in general make only 82 percent of what comparably employed men make (Department of Labor); and African-Americans make up 38 percent of the prison population despite representing only 13 percent of the total population.

By definition the problem is racism, misogyny, homophobia, elitism, and a total disregard for the environment and the science of climate change. But it is much more than that. All of these things are enabled by the abuse of power. Power is at the heart of our dying environment, our repression of women and minorities, growing inequities in wealth and opportunity, religious intolerance, our cultural divide, and the paralysis and malfeasance of our politicians and political institutions.

Specifically, we are failing because of the conventions our public and private institutions employ to define and allocate power. What we grossly mischaracterize as leadership is the raw and unbridled power that we have granted to the dark triad of psychology—the Machiavellians, narcissists, and psychopaths—among us.

It is not that these conventions, which helped to define the American Century, broke down or took a malevolent turn. They didn't. What happened is that the world itself changed. The context in which those conventions were designed and worked so well no longer exists. Our institutional conventions for the definition and allocation of power are not only misaligned with current reality—they are, in their very design, structured to maximize the pain and suffering that arises from the disconnect that arises in the current context.

We could, in other words, hardly do worse than we are now in aligning the conventions of power with the realities of the current world. Almost any change will be an improvement, and no change is guaranteed to take us down the road of disaster.

The source of the misalignment is actually pretty simple and straightforward. We have built our institutions on the supremacy of the individual. The common denominator to all of our freedom and opportunity in the United States, and in the West in general, is the self. We value nothing quite so much as we value the right to individual freedom, self-expression, and individual economic opportunity.

Herbert Hoover, thirty-first president of the United States, from 1929 to 1932, popularized the uniquely American notion of *rugged individualism*. It is the ideal behind the iconic American imagery of Wonder Woman and the Marlboro Man.

Horatio Alger, unleashed to pursue his dreams through the opportunities intrinsic to free-market capitalism, was free to claw his way to wealth and privilege through hard work and his very individual ingenuity. Alger is Atlas, the original Titan, as legendary mentor. It has always been the American way.

But the world that Atlas and Horatio have carried on their backs was always destined to become heavier. The passengers on our shared journey procreate, and the world gets more crowded. Mechanization fuels the Industrial Revolution, but the unintended consequence is a greater and greater division of labor that inevitably sets the stage for the exploitation of the workers, particularly when the capital it is built on resides in the hands of the few. Digital technology does to communication what mechanization did to labor. Only this time it happens in reverse. The informed few no longer tell us what to think. Information has been liberated. But yet another unintended consequence. With more came less—less truth, less trust, less transparency. The masses have not been freed; the dark triad has been empowered.

The duality of empowerment flows from the fact that power is a zero-sum game. You can't have more unless someone else has less. The result is a growing polarization on every front of culture, politics, and the economy.

The most obvious byproduct is that the rich are getting richer. There have always been people of wealth, of course. And there always will be. In the Soviet Union, communism, despite its promise of egalitarian utopia, ultimately failed to deliver. The allocation of power merely favored a new repressive elite. Never, however, has the wealth of the world been so concentrated as it is today. The global 1 percent now controls virtually half of all global wealth.

The nature of work itself has been polarized. In the digital universe, nothing is lost. Decisions, including the bad ones, are eternalized. If you have a job, you are harnessed to it. Personal downtime is a bitter anachronism. And if you don't have a job, the chances of finding one that fits your skills and experience are remote.

The benefit of the doubt is dead, too. We don't need it. We have Google and Facebook. According to the British Security Industry Association, there is something like five million active cameras in the public spaces of the United Kingdom today. By one estimate, there were seventeen thousand public security cameras in New York City alone by 2015. And that doesn't count the hackers and government agents who listen to our phone calls, watch us through our webcams, or steal our identities.

When President George W. Bush proclaimed, "You are either with us or against us," he could not have possibly imagined how true that would become. When we digitized our technology, we digitized our society, our politics, and our economy. There is no continuum. The spectrum of almost everything has been sliced into discrete data points. Never have we measured more things, like customer satisfaction and voter preferences, and never have the results been less meaningful.

Tolerance has died along with the continuum. Despite our rhetoric, people are routinely judged and allocated based on their race, gender, religion, sexual identity, and political values. Never before has our political discourse been less Socratic, less aspirational, or less civil. Righteous indignation, the close cousin of hatred, is the new standard of the decade.

Watching a network newscast today is like watching reruns of Jane Curtin and Dan Akroyd parodies of Shana Alexander and James Kilpatrick on *60 Minutes* "Point-Counterpoint" debates, but without the humor. It's like professional wrestling without the ropes.

Our social institutions, in general, have also decayed. In his book *Bowling Alone: The Collapse and Revival of American Community* (2000), Robert Putnam notes that attendance at the regular meetings of the country's leading service clubs, like Rotary and Kiwanis, declined by 58 percent in the period 1975–2000. Who has the time to participate? Or the interest? Or the sense of obligation?

Even our institutions of higher learning have followed the path of self-righteous indignation and intolerance, even though their path leads in a very different direction. They teach nothing quite so ardently today as they teach the fear of dissent and the right to be sheltered from differing opinions with which we might disagree.

Socrates is dead. There are only the voices that should be heard and those that should be silenced.

Our families have likewise lost their shared identity and sense of obligation. They are yet another casualty of the fragmentation of our labor, our identities, our legal rights, and our social and political discourse.

To date, any realization of the impact of the macro trends that engulf us has resulted in our doubling down on the conventions of the past—more personal rights and freedoms, less regulation, less obligation, and more protection from the voices we don't want to hear. The more we seek to strengthen the social, political, and economic conventions of individuality, however, the more we promote the deterioration we seek to escape. We merely raise the stakes. We add fuel to the fire.

We need to rethink and redefine the conventions themselves. The world we live in demands it. The world we have helped to define, but which, in turn, has defined us, as is the most fundamental law of nature, can no longer be managed, or even understood, in the images of Atlas and Horatio Alger, of Wonder Woman or the Marlboro Man, of the rugged individualist who leads us into battle like Teddy Roosevelt charging down San Juan Hill.

Self-control has never been a human strong suit. The evolutionary biologists and psychologists have a simple explanation. Self-control is seldom the obvious path to perpetuation of the species. It is the proactive self, the capital "I," the healthiest, strongest, and fastest "Me" that we honor and elevate. It is the richest, the most beautiful, and the most famous that we envy and imitate.

Corporate CEOs have been acknowledging the injustice of executive compensation for decades. But what have they done about it? Less than nothing.

Celebrities have voiced their disillusionment over their shallow fame for even longer. Hollywood, however, is more openly active in politics than it has ever been. *Keeping Up With the Kardashians*, built on the superficial accomplishment of fame alone, has been a smash hit for more than a decade and a new contract, rumored to be the largest in the history of reality television, has reportedly been inked to extend it another five years.

Americans, in general, have been decrying racism and misogyny for at least three generations now, depending on how you define generations. Black Lives Matter, the #MeToo campaign, and Occupy Wall Street are only recent expressions of frustration and failure.

What gives? (I'm told nobody says that anymore, but I have faith in my readers.)

What gives is that we must turn our conventions for the definition and allocation of power on their heads. What gives is that we need to rewire supremacy itself from the "I" to the "We." We need to stop thinking about the self and start thinking about the collective us.

And this, unfortunately, is where I will lose many of you. "The communists had their day. The socialists had their day. And they all failed." You've already thought it, even if you haven't said it out loud.

Your objections are irrefutable. The few remaining communist states virtually all boast relatively free market economies. And no socialist state has yet replicated the influential vitality of what de Tocqueville called "the American experiment." None.

But virtually all the "isms" we have known to date have merely been variations on a central and consistent theme. Every -ism starts with the letter I." Virtually every form of political and economic paradigm to date has been built on the same convention—*I Shall Master*. Every model has been built on the back of the individual.

The only difference has been the methodology for dividing up the spoils. In one case, "I create, and I keep," and in the other, "I create, and you take away."

What we need today, however, is a model of "We create, and we willingly and enthusiastically apply toward the common good, both individually and communally." We don't need to double down on socialism or communism. We need to create a new form of political, social, and economic organization. I call it We-ism.

Yes, it is still an "ism." It still starts with I. That can't be helped. Language is a human convention we created for the purpose of enhancing the effectiveness and the efficiency of our communication. It is no surprise, therefore, that we constructed language in our own image and reflective of our own limitations. The elevation of language to something more than an artificial convention is what has given us political correctness. If we redefine the conventions with which we define and allocate power, we will need to redefine the conventions of language anyway. But it's not a priority.

What is a priority is to redefine the conventions of power, not to subdue the individual, but to redirect it toward the shared, collective reality in which we now exist. We must not thwart individualism so much as we need to harness it in the interest of collaboration and collective progress.

The recognition that we exist within an integrated, interconnected, tightly woven tapestry of forces and influences has been the most far-reaching and meaningful realization of the modern world. What Newton saw as a single apple falling from a single tree is now known to be part of a much larger gravitational force, the influence of which is felt at the farthest reaches of the universe.

We no longer have psychology. We have developmental psychology, neuropsychology, evolutionary psychology, and economic psychology. The most powerful knowledge, we now know, exists not within a discipline, but in the overlap that exists between all disciplines of knowledge and discovery.

The most progressive and successful companies operate not as a collection of independent functional staffs, but as collaborative teams encompassing a wide array of specialized knowledge and skills. The division of function has given way to the division of task.

Our politics are no longer defined by monolithic parties but by coalitions of very specific identity and interests.

We-ism, thankfully, is both necessary and attractive. It is as much a reversion to what we've always held dear as it is a departure from a glorious past. There has always been a contradiction between our stated ideals and the reality we embraced. We aspired to be the Marlboro Man, but no one ever really liked the gunner on the basketball team, the social butterfly in high school with the posse of affected snobs, or the office braggart. We've admired the elite only to the extent that we believed that we, too, could be one of them.

More than anything else, the American dream is a dream state built on fair play and equal opportunity. The great melting pot of American immigration was not a process of swapping one identity for another; it was a process whereby a new identity was created, an identity built on mutual respect and fairness. No immigrant ever signed on to assimilated poverty, repression, and discrimination.

As has always been true, but not always acknowledged, humanity, however we came into existence, is but one facet or expression of nature. And nature, as we have learned environmentally, is a giant ecosystem of interconnected causes and effects. Nothing happens in isolation. No one facet of nature exists independently of the world around it. A tree is defined by its soil, air, climate, altitude, and a host of other variables. The trees of a forest, scientists have now learned, actually communicate in their own fundamental way in order to promote the collective interest of the forest.

An article by Dutch correspondent Rutger Bregman, published by the World Economic Forum on April 12, 2017, stated: "A growing number of people think their job is useless. Time to rethink the meaning of work." In his article, translated by Elizabeth Manton, Bregman cites a 2013 survey of twelve thousand professionals by the *Harvard Business Review*. Half said that they felt their jobs had no "meaning and significance." Another poll cited by Bregman reached out to 230,000 employees in 142 countries. In that study only 13 percent indicated they found *any* satisfaction in their work.

Corporations have spent billions of dollars training and motivating their employees, redesigning the work environment to make it more egalitarian and collaborative, and strengthening their talent management and retention efforts. By any measure, however, it isn't working.

It isn't working because we haven't changed the fundamental convention of how we allocate power. We've wrapped the organizational hierarchy in bright new colors and aspirational language, but the convention remains. In fact, we've strengthened the hierarchy through disparate pay schemes and codified elitism, hollowing out the core of what the convention relies upon to work.

We've gutted our business institutions of trust and the sense of obligation that naturally flows from it. There are plenty of posters on the wall or adorning the home page of the employee portal attesting to some variation of, "Our employees are our greatest asset." But it's a lie.

Every employee knows that at the first sign of a bad quarter, he or she could be gone. Employees know that the boss will throw them under the bus the first time his or her own job or advancement is at risk. Every employee knows that the real aim of talent management is to cull out the people who don't exhibit the right political allegiance or who otherwise dare to challenge the emperor.

It wasn't always this way. The doctrine of "employment at will" has long defined the legal standard by which employees held their jobs. Until the 1980s, however, and the opioid of globalism emerged as the corporate and political cause célèbre, employment at will was subordinate to the informal but very real contract of employer obligation. Employees weren't assets to be traded or jettisoned at the whim of executives posturing for their own self-interests. Leaders had obligations to the workers and the community that far outweighed their right to exercise their power in their own self-interests.

There was no debate about the work-life balance because the very existence of the distinction was a sign of failure. If your work was not giving your life purpose, there was a presumed failure of leadership.

There are many cultures around the world where obligation remains a powerful standard and motivator. And, on balance, these are always the countries that are declared the happiest or where the quality of life is the highest and most complete.

More than anything else, We-ism, as I will come to define it in this book, is a system of obligation. Some of it can and should be formalized. But it can unfold over time. I am not advocating revolution. I reject all violence.

But I do advocate change. I advocate for the supremacy of our common humanity. I advocate for a world that honors the individual and gives all people the opportunity to expand their wings and rise as high as their talents and hard work can take them. I only advocate that they never lose sight of the ground from whence they rose. They may, by definition, not be able to rise as high, but the view will be far more beautiful and exhilarating.

Summary

We must realign the conventions we employ to define and allocate power to put the collective "We" before the individual "I." I call it We-ism.

- Our leaders in every sphere of our politics, our society, and our economics must put obligation above self-interest by defining self-interest as obligation.
- We must recognize that individual advancement without collective advancement is hollow and unsustainable.
- We must recognize that the universe is not a collection of independent, discrete parts, but a holistic, integrated organism whose life and soul is defined by the balance among its discrete parts.

CHAPTER 2

Change

• • •

Government of the people, by the people, for the people.

—Abraham Lincoln
Gettysburg Address, 1863

From the beginning, the United States has been all about the people. The Bill of Rights, with its emphasis on our inalienable privileges and personal liberties, is at the heart of our politics. The fruit of our labor, earned in an efficient free market, is the foundation of our economy. Unlocking our individual potential and creativity is at the heart of our education. And the freedom to be at one with the Creator, however we choose to define what that means, is at the heart of our religion.

"The people," in other words, on whose shoulders and for whose benefit the American experiment was undertaken, has always been known and understood through the lens of the self. We have individual rights, individual freedoms, the individual right to a trial by a jury of individual peers, the right to individual expression, and the right to the individual pursuit of happiness. We are a nation of rugged individualists, as Herbert Hoover often put it, immortalized by the imagery of John Wayne, Wonder Woman, and the Marlboro Man.

The advice to "pursue your dreams," "celebrate your individuality," and "be yourself" have defined a social, political, and economic context within which America emerged from its original thirteen colonies, characterized by the language and imagery of self. Self-reliance, self-determination, and self-pleasure have put "I" at the center of what it means to be an Amer"I"can.

The perspective has served us well. We are the most prosperous nation in the history of the world. We are the most powerful nation on the face of the planet. Our democratic freedoms are without equal. We boast many of the world's best universities, the most advanced technology, the strongest military, and the most robust and comprehensive financial markets that humanity has ever known.

The history of America is a testament to individualism, and it's worked splendidly:

- In 2014, more than 67,000 individuals graduated with a PhD in the United States, more than twice the number of its nearest rival, Germany, and thirty times the number earned in Russia.
- The United States, with 336, has more Nobel laureates than any other country, including 94 in physiology or medicine alone. The United States leads all other countries, in fact, in every Nobel discipline except literature, where France, Germany, and the United Kingdom have performed better.
- Of the major developed economies, the United States generates the most GDP both in aggregate and per capita. The per capita rate is 19 percent higher than Germany's and 35 percent higher than that of the United Kingdom.

- The United States is home to 565 billionaires, more than China, Germany, and India, the next three by count, combined.
- The United States is the only country to have put a person on the moon and the first to break the sound barrier. (Chuck Yeager did it in 1947.)
- At $150 billion per year, the United States exports more food than any other country in the world, accounting for roughly 10 percent of the world's food production.
- While the United States has the third largest pool of Internet users, behind China and India, its penetration is higher at 88 percent. (Penetration in China and India is 53 percent and 34 percent, respectively.)
- The United States has won a total of 2,804 medals at the Olympic Summer and Winter Games, more than twice the former Soviet Union, accounting for 15 percent of all medals awarded despite only representing 5 percent of the world's population.
- According to *Fortune* the United States is home to 132 of the top 500 companies in the world, measured by revenue; the most of any country.

It is a record of achievement unequaled in human history. It is a record of grit, perseverance, and American ingenuity on every front. But above all else, it is the record of an unrivaled, unapologetic belief in the power and dignity of the common man and woman.

And, yet, despite all of this admirable success, our greatest doubts, our greatest blunders, and our greatest failings, are likewise deeply personal:

- We have the largest prison population and the highest incarceration rate in the world. And according to statistics

provided by the NAACP, in 2014 African Americans constituted 34 percent of the correctional population. In total, African Americans are incarcerated at more than five times the rate of whites, and, according to the *Washington Post*, one in every nine African American children has had a parent behind bars.
- Our health-care costs are the highest in the world, but we are the only developed nation without universal health insurance.
- We produce more greenhouse gases than any other country, again in both absolute and relative terms.
- Life expectancy in the United States, at seventy-nine, ranks only 53rd in the world, behind Germany (28th), France (14th), and the United Kingdom (29th), even though the United States spends more on health care per capita ($9,200 per person per year) than any other country.
- At 5.80 deaths per 1,000 births, the infant mortality rate in the United States is higher than the European Union (4.00), Canada (4.50), South Korea (3.00), and Japan (2.00).
- Despite its wealth, the United States ranks 14th in the UN's World Happiness Report, below Australia (9th), Canada (7th), and Norway (1st).
- According to data from the Organization for Economic Cooperation and Development (OECD) for 2014, income inequality, as measured by the Gini coefficient, is higher in the United States than all other countries except Turkey, Mexico, and Costa Rica.
- Ranked by the 2017 Mid-Year Crime Index reported by Numbeo.com, the United States (48.50) ranked 44th out of 110 countries, higher than Russia (45.70), Turkey (41.03), the Philippines (40.04), and China (32.49).

- According to the Corruption Perceptions Index (2016) developed by Transparency International, the United States ranked 18th, behind Canada, Germany, the United Kingdom, Australia, and Hong Kong. (Denmark and New Zealand tied for 1st.)
- According to the OEDC Violence against Women Indicator for 2014, the United States ranks higher than the United Kingdom, Spain, Sweden, Canada, Netherlands, Italy, and France.
- According to the US Census Bureau, forty-five million Americans, or 14.5 percent, were living in poverty as recently as 2013, the last year for which hard data is available.

Why? What is the basis for this disconnect between personal accomplishment and personal failure?

In a word, we are the victims of our own success. Our scientific, technological, educational, and economic advances have redefined the world in which we live. And these factors have redefined it to a degree that has not only transformed the world, but has redefined social, political, and economic cause and effect.

It is a transformation that has both caused, and been caused by, profound changes in the context in which our economic, political, and social institutions exist and operate.

Consider this small sampling of facts:

- There were 2.5 million people living in the United States in 1776. There are 315 million people here today.
- The entire landmass of the original thirteen colonies was 339,000 square miles. The United States today covers 3,678,000 square miles.

- The only guns available when the Second Amendment was ratified in 1791 were the single-fire musket and the flintlock pistol. In the hands of the most skilled operators, they had a capacity of about three rounds per minute and were accurate only at very short distances. The 2017 Las Vegas shooter, who killed 58 and left 546 injured, by comparison, was able to fire 1,100 rounds in less than ten minutes, massacring innocent civilians at a range of almost 500 yards.
- The first train locomotive to run on US rails did not go into operation until 1829. The first American car was not built until 1893. The first commercial flight did not take place until 1914.
- The pharmaceutical industry, as we know it today, did not come into existence until the mid-twentieth century.
- The Internet has been in widespread existence for less than thirty years.
- The Sixteenth Amendment, legalizing the income tax and creating a powerful tool for social and economic engineering, was not ratified until 1913. The tax system we know today did not come into existence until 1954.
- Only 2 percent of Americans live on farms or ranches today. In 1790, 90 percent of us did.

What does it all mean?

For starters, it means that the relative isolation and independence we have known in the past no longer exists. We live together, work together, and socialize in closer proximity, real and digital, than ever before. While we may know less about our neighbors, we know more about virtually everyone else. We are literally drowning in information about the people and the world around us.

We know what our Internet celebrities ate for breakfast. We know exactly what some unknown man or woman halfway across the world looked like before and after shedding one hundred pounds by eating nothing but ice cream. We can track the exact location of our children in real time. The answer to any question is only a click away. We don't even have to get up from the couch; we can just ask Alexa or Siri.

Our privacy has been shattered. Thieves steal our identities or hold them for ransom. Governments watch and listen. Intimate pictures meant for two eyes are seen by millions. Marketers know exactly where we live and the red shoes we looked at last week have been following us around the Internet ever since. The stupid stuff we say in the heat of the moment never goes away, the record etched in a cloud we cannot see or touch.

There is, however, a duality to the universe. For every pro there is a con. For light there is shadow. For fire there is water. For cold there is hot. It is the price extracted by a natural order that exists as a vast ecosystem that demands nothing quite so vehemently as it demands balance.

We have, however, overshot that mark. Our single-minded pursuit of the self has, largely through the transformative power of technology, created a disconnect between our ideals and our reality. We manage our world with a perspective, and the rules built upon it, that no longer reflects our reality.

There is no place in this new world for Wonder Woman or the Marlboro Man. There is only room for the Facebook circle of friends, the self-replicating tweet, and the viral meme. The personal is now the public. The confidante is now the coterie.

Which is precisely why the rules and conventions developed almost 250 years ago, and refined, expanded, and further protected ever since, simply don't work anymore. However we want to think of ourselves, we are a collectivist nation. We just don't behave like one. Most of us, in fact, don't want to be one.

But here we are.

In the pages that follow, I will look more closely at each of the three primary spheres of influence that define our collective experience: the economic, social, and political. I will examine what has changed and what the implications of that change are.

In the end, I will offer some ideas on how to move forward. These ideas, however, are not meant to be all-inclusive or exclusive. I am not a prophet and make no false pretense to be. I am also not a scholar as the academics among us define that term. I have training in economics and business, and a lifetime of experience, both here in the United States and abroad. I have no suffix after my name, however. And that will matter to some. It shouldn't, but it matters greatly to many, but not all, of those who have the suffix. It's another testament to our infatuation with the self. "I am, you are not."

I have not followed the historical scholarly standard for annotation, either. And I haven't done so for one simple reason: It is largely a waste of time and paper in today's digital world. Annotation was developed for a time and place when you had to go to a library to look at books and microfiche to verify facts or look at source material. Today we have Google, and it is far cleverer that Dewey's decimal system ever was. Every fact or quote I state here should be easily verifiable with a flick of the wrist.

With that, let's move forward.

Summary

The United States is a very different place than it was almost 250 years ago. It's bigger, more crowded, and far more technologically advanced. And while we have known a great deal of success, we have also failed to achieve some of our most important ideals relating to equality and justice.

PART I
Economic
• • •

CHAPTER 3

Division of Labor

• • •

The division of labour, however, so far as it can be introduced, occasions, in every art, a proportionable increase of the productive powers of labour.

—Adam Smith
The Wealth of Nations, 1776

While Adam Smith, the man most closely associated with the free-market capitalism on which the American economic system is modeled, is best known for the "invisible hand" of self-interest that guides economic efficiency and production, it is his emphasis on the division of labor that is at the heart of the American economic model. That invisible hand belongs to an individual, and each individual has unique knowledge, experience, and talent that separate his or her hand from all others.

If each of us labors at that which we are best trained and suited for, our collective productivity will be maximized on every front. We will produce the best products of the best quality at the lowest possible price. What else could we hope for from our economic system?

Nothing, actually. That has always been the goal, and should remain the goal, of our economic engine. From a purely economic perspective, that raison d'être has not changed. What has changed is the context in which it operates.

The division of labor premise is built, like any other premise, on a foundation of assumptions. First among them is the assumption that the market for labor is itself efficient. It assumes that talent can be known and the knowledge of that knowing shared.

And at one time that was a pretty safe assumption. Our jobs were pretty simple. It didn't take too much training to be a competent blacksmith or candlemaker. Farming is a bit more complicated, but most people had been learning the craft from birth. And we needed engineers, but not too many of them. There were no space stations, and our fuel was largely confined to wood, coal, and whale oil. Even science and medicine were in their infancy. Most jobs, it can be fairly safely assumed, were within the natural abilities of most people. However labor was divided, there was probably someone available to fill the job.

And since we lived and worked in largely localized environments, it wasn't hard to identify the best candidate for each job. Everybody in a community pretty much knew who the best carpenter was, the best marksman, and the most competent at building and fixing the few mechanical devices in existence.

Even New York City had only twenty-five thousand residents in 1776. They certainly didn't all know one another, but it wouldn't have been too hard to sort out who was the most qualified, or competently qualified, for each job, none of which, outside of the arts, were all that specialized. And if you heard about someone who was reputed to be good at whatever job need you had in the next neighborhood over, you could get on your horse and go find him or her without much effort or time invested.

But that's all changed, of course. The array of jobs it takes to staff the modern economy is much broader and more varied. We no longer need blacksmiths; we need programmers in 5-axis CNC machining. We don't need farmers; we need agriculture specialists who understand chemistry, botany, and meteorology. We don't need typists; we need people who can code Java or Python.

Few of these jobs are learned from our parents. In my own generation, many jobs required a college degree. Many jobs now, however, require a graduate or postgraduate degree and years of development and training. Some jobs are so specialized that there is only a handful of people who have the natural skills and the acquired knowledge to fill them.

As a result, the local labor pool is insufficient to find qualified job applicants. For all but the most menial jobs, which are largely disappearing as automation and artificial intelligence (AI) surge past the tipping point, the search for Adam Smith's talented labor must be regional, or even global, in scope.

That, in turn, has put a premium on our ability to identify and quantify talent. We no longer know who is the best marksman or farmer. We must have a way to both objectively evaluate skills and talents and to communicate those findings efficiently and completely. And the more specialized labor becomes, the bigger that challenge is.

And the reality is that we are not rising to that challenge very successfully. Our ability to define the most talented nuclear physicist or molecular biologist is limited by the conventions of assessment we employ. We are forced to rely on standardized proxies of assessment that may be more coincidental than causal, particularly when the skills required for a job are difficult to articulate in easily measurable terms.

In fact, we frequently revert back to the very subjective judgment of the village. Experts suggest that as many as 90 percent of the senior executive positions filled in the United States each year are, in the end, granted to someone personally known by someone with access to the decision-maker. In theory, this gives the process added credibility because it considers intangible skills and personal qualities that don't show up in a résumé or interview. In practice, however, the assessment may have been formed and passed along on the thinnest of evidence.

The proof, as they say, is in the pudding. The expected tenure of a corporate CEO in the United States today is only three years. And this poor record of selection performance has occurred despite extensive advances in quantitative assessment and a much greater ability among executive recruiters to scour the universe for candidates.

At the end of the day, the hiring process today is a roll of the dice. The knowledge necessary to make Smith's division of labor productive simply doesn't exist. And further development of technology along any observable path is not going to help. Most such technological developments to date have empowered communication but have had little impact on our objective ability to assess talent. And while AI may eventually revolutionize the assessment process, such breakthroughs are well off into the future.

Does this mean we should stop genuflecting at Smith's altar to the division of labor? At one level, there is resounding evidence that the answer is yes.

Manufacturers realized long ago that the functional division of labor minimized direct labor costs, but at a steep price in the capital costs of inventory and storage and the ability to maximize quality and improve response time. Many factories were reorganized, as a result, and functionally defined layouts were transformed into process or product-defined layouts, where workers, cross-trained in all of the functional jobs required to build a product or provide a service, took ownership of a product or process from beginning to end.

With automation and AI, however, those are the jobs that are disappearing from our economic landscape. The jobs left behind often take knowledge that takes longer to acquire and skill set combinations that are less common in the population of potential job applicants.

It is a challenge that has been greatly exaggerated by the more complete understanding that has been driven and accelerated by technology. In the sciences and in medicine, our acquisition of knowledge has unveiled the significant degree to which our world, and the building blocks that define it, are interrelated and interconnected. To understand economics, we must understand human psychology. To understand biology, we must understand the role and impact of evolution. To understand climate change, we must know far more than meteorology or atmospheric chemistry.

The key in all areas of employment today is cross-functional knowledge and utility and the ability to collaborate. While jobs have become more specialized, the ability to work with others has never been more essential. Both requirements, in turn and collectively, have further enhanced the challenge of identifying the most talented among us and slotting the right person into the right job.

This challenge, moreover, is in direct conflict with another defining development of the times—career mobility. Young people entering the workplace today are being told that they can expect to have five or six different employers over the course of their careers. And, they are being told, in addition to being a reality of the shareholder supremacy that drives most corporate behavior, and which I will discuss in detail in a future chapter, this is a good thing.

But is it? Can you collaborate more efficiently with a team you've just met and whose trust you don't share? Is your knowledge and expertise truly transferable, or are there nuances to each company and each process that have to be learned? Is it good for your own personal well-being to uproot your family and move to a new community every few years, or does that just contribute to feelings of alienation and loneliness?

In theory, of course, collaboration can be taught, and there are plenty of experts making a very good living teaching it. And the theoretical case can be made that the knowledge specific to a company or process is as likely to be bad knowledge as good knowledge. In the mind-set of modern business, perhaps people do things a certain way because that's all they've ever known.

When I began my corporate career in the 1970s, companies valued nothing quite so highly as they valued loyalty. With rare exceptions, if you had worked for three different companies in the first decade of your career, the most prestigious companies would avoid you like the plague. They had psychological profiling back then, of course, and functional knowledge was no more difficult to assess than it is today. Companies had learned from experience, however, that nothing mattered quite so much as loyalty, in part because the division of labor was, in fact, already accelerating and the universities were not keeping up. The most valuable training most people received was acquired on the job. And no company wanted to make a big investment in developing your skills only to have you take them elsewhere.

That, of course, is considered myopic thinking today. Many companies believe that with job specialization has come enhanced standardization. Skills are easily transferable, and collaboration is a process that is independent of the players involved. Or should be.

That, however, is not the reality. I have managed dozens, if not hundreds, of teams over the course of my career, and not one—not once—did the team walk through the door ready to collaborate productively and efficiently. And those teams, without a single exception, were more effective and productive after one year than they were after one week, and better after two years than they were after one.

Similarly, I have been in hundreds, if not thousands of manufacturing plants around the world. And I have yet to find any two that are truly identical in the ways that really matter in terms of cost, quality, and flexibility. Even the most ardent competitors, whose products the marketplace is literally unable to distinguish between, arrived at that commonality along largely different paths.

No corporate practice, in my lifetime, has been more destructive to long-term corporate health than the natural selection process popularized by Jack Welch and GE. The idea that you should constantly cull out the weakest members of the herd is the most myopic and irrational policy a company can possibly follow.

It assumes, for starters, that you can identify who those weak performers are. You can't. And even if you could, it assumes that the skills your organization requires today are the ones it will require tomorrow. This is not the current reality, and it is becoming less and less realistic with each passing year and each technological innovation.

It ignores, moreover, fundamental human dynamics and psychology. What has been the strongest organizational unit throughout all of time? It's the family. And would you cull your children every year in the interest of family performance?

We have to stop thinking of our organizations, corporate or otherwise, as a collection of divided laborers. That may have been practical in eighteenth-century England, where Adam Smith developed his theories. It is not practical—in fact it is destructive—in twenty-first century America.

The division of labor is an anachronism in an integrated world where economic value is created collectively, not individually. The most specialized jobs are both the easiest to mechanize and create only limited economic value in isolation.

Unfortunately, the governance systems employed by most corporations and employers today are designed to promote and maintain Smith's Holy Grail. While there have been efforts to recognize the importance of teamwork and collaboration, the basic structure of most organizations, and the talent systems used to manage them, are of limited effectiveness and, in fact, promote the turnover at the heart of decay in our performance-obsessed economy.

Summary

The capitalist model is built on the division of labor. That made sense during industrialization, but it is ineffective, if not counterproductive, in an integrated digital economy.

- Organizations should be restructured not to be hierarchical or flat, but unstructured, organic, and constantly adapting to the ever-changing environment.
- Motivational and development systems should promote retention as much as they promote individual performance. Financial incentives alone won't be enough. Organizations must learn to appeal to broader and more deeply held personal needs and desires relating to the desire for development and the need for connection.
- We must break down the white patriarchal model of power. Gender, racial, and other forms of inclusion will not be realized until we do. The abuse of power, whether conscious or not, is at the heart of all organizational imbalance and inappropriate behavior.

CHAPTER 4

Corporate Personhood

• • •

> All persons born or naturalized in the United States and subject to the jurisdiction thereof, are citizens of the United States and of the State wherein they reside. No State shall make or enforce any law which shall abridge the privileges or immunities of citizens of the United States; nor shall any State deprive any person of life, liberty, or property, without due process of law; nor deny to any person within its jurisdiction the equal protection of the laws.
>
> —FOURTEENTH AMENDMENT (PARTIAL)
> US CONSTITUTION, 1868

THE MODERN CORPORATION CAN TRACE its roots back to the Middle Ages, when the British king formally recognized English towns as independent entities in the eyes of the law. The first commercial corporations were later chartered by the monarchy to further the economic interests of the crown. Queen Elizabeth, for example, chartered the British East India Company in 1600 to challenge the Dutch-Portuguese monopoly on the spice trade.

The American colonies borrowed the idea, and colonial legislatures chartered corporations to build canals, bridges, and roads and to pursue other economic endeavors in the public interest. Each corporation was chartered for a specific purpose and for a specific period of time.

In a series of rulings rarely studied by schoolchildren, however, the US Supreme Court, starting with its 1819 ruling in *Trustees of Dartmouth College v. Woodward*, gradually chipped away at government control over the corporations the states chartered. The modern era of self-defined corporate purpose fully materialized with the 1886 US Supreme Court ruling in *Santa Clara County v. Southern Pacific Railroad*. Invoking, by inference, the Fourteenth Amendment to the US Constitution—the "due process" amendment designed to protect emancipated slaves—the court ruled that a corporation is a "person," with all the constitutional rights and protections, save voting, enjoyed by individuals.

In 1952, the US Supreme Court formally extended those rights to include the right to free expression as guaranteed by the First Amendment. The court was ruling in a case filed by a film distributor after the New York State Board of Regents refused to allow the public showing of a film by Federico Fellini, called *The Miracle*, after deeming it sacrilegious.

In 1976, moreover, the Supreme Court expanded the First Amendment protection granted to business by creating the "commercial speech doctrine." The doctrine, articulated in the *Virginia Pharmacy Board* decision struck down the power of any court to regulate marketing and advertising claims, essentially granting wide latitude to ignore or circumvent regulations relating to consumer disclosure, privacy protection, and ingredient labeling.

And, of course, in 2009 the US Supreme Court gutted the country's first legitimate attempt at campaign finance reform, the McCain-Feingold Act, in *Citizens United*, ruling that corporations had the right to fund, with no quantitative restrictions, political advertising.

In contemporary politics, of course, free speech is not free. By the numbers, in granting the right to unlimited political spending to corporations, the court essentially silenced the American citizen in the same way that, as we will see in a later chapter, the legal doctrine of employment at will, under the guise of preventing indentured servitude, gutted employee protections.

The practical effect of corporate personhood, as it is currently defined and protected, is nothing short of the complete perversion of the very ideals of political democracy. The moneyed elite, who control both Wall Street and the board room, granting them effective control over the political process but also empowering them to hire the best and brightest advertising teams to, in the name of free speech, sell us products that we don't need, now control an effective closed loop of power.

It's a classic case of money begets power and power begets more money. We have created a virtual perpetual motion machine of power that permanently raises the drawbridge on the masses in the same way that the feudal lords of Europe once did.

It's more than a feudal system, with the corporation as feudal lord and the common citizen as powerless vassal. It is a closed loop of power destined to accumulate more and more power until it either bursts or implodes. It's a dystopian state on a scale that even Orwell himself could not have imagined.

Consider that, according to statista.com, the United States spent $195 billion on advertising media buys in 2016. That does not include the money spent on creating those advertisements. But even the media buy is more than the GDP of twenty of the fifty US states combined. It's also more than the combined profits of the eight most profitable companies in the United States, according to *Fortune*, and four times the total profits of the country's most profitable company, Apple.

Roughly one-third of that amount, of course, is funded by US taxpayers since it's all tax deductible. And what, exactly, are they getting in return? Will Americans starve if they aren't reminded that there are grocery stores where they can procure food? Will they lose their jobs out of ignorance of the fact that they can buy a car in order to get to work? Will they be unaware that there is medicine for erectile dysfunction if they don't see the advertisement during *Monday Night Football*?

Speaking of the NFL, according to research gathered by CNN, NFL teams sell between $1.5 billion to $2 billion worth of luxury and high-end club seats per year, and, "Almost all suites and club tickets are bought by corporate clients, which write the cost off as a business entertainment expense" (money.cnn.com; 1/30/2015; by Chris Isidore). This, the NFL, is an organization that paid its own CEO/commissioner more than $34 million in 2014, funded, in part, of course, by US taxpayers.

Among the most highly compensated CEOs of 2014, however, such largesse would not have put NFL Commissioner Goodell in the top ten. He would have ranked only nineteenth according to the *New York Times*, well below the top dog, the CEO of Discovery Communications, which owns the Discovery Channel, who was awarded $156 million as his just reward for the year.

This, of course, is income, not wealth. The ten wealthiest Americans, all men, on the 2017 Forbes 400, control roughly $610 billion in wealth, an amount greater than the GDP of Sweden. Six of the ten are household names and made their money taking tech companies public. Only three run private companies, other than to manage their personal investments.

A good portion of that wealth, of course, as is true of the wealth of virtually all of the wealthy elite, would never have materialized if it weren't for something called intellectual property and the rights to it granted to corporations and individuals.

Intellectual property law dates back to medieval Europe, although it was originally used to give guilds, or associations of artisans, monopoly power over a given industry. In that way it inhibited creativity and innovation as much as it promoted it.

Thanks to Article 1, Section 8 of the US Constitution, intellectual property is the domain of the US federal government, not the states. It now covers trademarks, copyrights, patents, industrial design rights, and in some jurisdictions, trade secrets.

The purpose of intellectual property laws is to spur innovation. The government recognizes that some innovation requires a substantial upfront investment, and the investor must have a reasonable expectation that the investment can be recouped in the marketplace. Given the core purpose of promoting progress, however, protection has, until recently, been narrowly defined and of limited duration.

In recent decades, however, corporations and individuals have come to view intellectual property rights as financial assets rather than a mechanism for recouping the costs of developing innovation. In 2013, the US Patent & Trademark Office estimated that intellectual property in the United States held a value of more than $5 trillion and created incremental employment for approximately 18 million Americans.

While corporations continue to lobby for broader and stronger intellectual property protection, particularly in the international arena, there is a growing chorus of progressive voices who believe we have taken the concept too far. Their argument has both practical and moral components.

The larger legal issue turns on the obvious question—where does innovation come from? It obviously comes from individuals, but where do they find it? Ideas don't just germinate out of thin air. They start someplace. And who can say where that is?

As an author, for example, I sit at my computer and type out words that float through my conscious thought. Those words, however, originate in, and are shaped by, the thousands and thousands of experiences I have had throughout my life, many of which were strongly influenced, if not defined, by someone else. To what extent are the ideas of my parents, my former teachers, and my former bosses and colleagues given dimension through what to me feels like an independent process of creation?

To what extent, in fact, can anyone have a truly original idea? While the great novelists of our time are undoubtedly more creative writers than the rest of us, they must ultimately write about things in the real world. A poet may compose a very creative poem about trains, for example, that virtually no one else has the talent to create. But where would the poet be without trains in the first place? Which, of course, the poet did not invent.

The stakes, of course, are getting higher at a time when creativity is far less fungible and tangible and seldom exists independently. The Mona Lisa exists unto itself, but what is an app without the device it is designed to run on? What is a million lines of creative software code without a server to process it? Where does the horizon end and the sky begin? And what is one without the other?

To what extent, moreover, do developed countries have a moral right to deprive poorer, less technically competent countries from access to technology that would greatly reduce hardship and suffering? Do individuals deserve to suffer simply because they have less education or capital to procure intellectual property from its owner?

And even if we look only at our own self-interests, have we not determined that the earth's climate is a collective global asset? If we have technology that can help control global warming, is it really in our interests to withhold it for purely financial reasons?

The precedent for the broader sharing of intellectual capital, in fact, is already there. Much of the research that has been critical to the advancement of technology has been funded by the federal government at taxpayer expense. The National Institute of Health spends more than $30 billion per year funding groundbreaking research in biotechnology and pharmacology that is subsequently commercialized, at little cost, by private industry.

An article in the *Harvard Business Review* by Mariana Mazzucato, dated March 8, 2013, states: "Many of the revolutionary technologies that make the iPhone and other products and services 'smart' were funded by the US government. Take, for instance, the Internet, GPS, touchscreen display, as well as the latest voice-activated personal assistant, Siri. And Apple did not just benefit from government-funded research activities. It also received its early stage finance from the US government's Small Business Investment Company." Yet it was Apple's management, and the venture capitalists that swooped in after the initial risks of the startup were in the rearview mirror, that profited from Apple's record-breaking financial windfall. If anything, Apple, like most corporations, has gone out of its way to avoid paying US taxes and reimbursing US taxpayers for their initial investment.

Google has similarly gained at taxpayer expense. The algorithm at the heart of its dominant search engine was originally funded by the Nation Science Foundation. And Google, like Apple, has used complex tax structures designed to manipulate legislative oversights in the Internal Revenue Code to avoid paying taxes on overseas income.

Not only are the tech companies not paying the taxpayers a fair market value for their research, they are essentially forcing those same taxpayers to fund intellectual property litigation, and acquisition in lieu of litigation, to the tune of, according to research out of Stanford University, another $20 billion per year, all of which is, conveniently for them, tax deductible.

The taxpayer largesse, of course, extends well beyond Silicon Valley. NASA maintains a running list of all of the technology it has transferred to the private sector over the years. It's an impressive and comprehensive list that impacts the lives of every American in ways they are probably not aware of. The development of infrared ear thermometers, artificial limbs, anti-icing and chemical detection systems for aircraft, advanced gear to protect firefighters, enriched baby food, portable cordless vacuums, and the technology for freeze-drying food are just a few examples provided by NASA itself.

Funding basic scientific research is a function ideally suited to the public sector, tying in, as it does, with the work of public research universities and other institutions. It's hard to think of a more efficient and practical way to fund such research, improving the lives of all Americans and maintaining our ability to shelter, feed, protect, and employ our collective population.

Few people would suggest, moreover, that the government try to commercialize its own research. That, the world knows from experience, is not an ideal role for government to play unless absolutely necessary.

It seems beyond rational debate, however, that the taxpayers should not enjoy at least some of the financial windfall that comes from its research investment. The only way to justify the current situation is if the financial and commercial markets are truly efficient in the purest theoretical fashion. And we know they are not.

How can the value of Tesla, which sold 76,000 vehicles in 2016 and lost $675 million, and is expected to burn through more than $12 million in cash *per day* in 2017, be worth more than Ford, a proven company that sold 2.6 million vehicles and earned $4.6 billion? That's only efficient if, in fact, the meteoritic growth narrative that Tesla has fed to investors comes true. Of course it may, but so may I live to the age of two hundred. (I'm not betting my Tesla stock on it.)

Summary
At the end of the day, corporation are not people, and we should stop treating them like they are.

- Corporations should be financially banned from the political arena. Period, no exceptions.
- Corporations should not enjoy unfettered freedom of speech, particularly when it comes to selling us products and services that we don't need and that have no redeeming economic or social value.
- Intellectual property laws should be rewritten to deny protection where it infringes on material social and economic progress, both locally and globally, and protection, under any circumstances, should be limited to actual cost recovery.
- Taxpayers should be reimbursed for their research and intellectual property to the same extent inventors and private investors are.

CHAPTER 5

Corporate Ownership

• • •

I'm only in this for the money.

—Attributed to Carl Icahn
Jeff Gramm
Business Insider, 6/16/2016

If the division of labor is the engine of wealth creation in Adam Smith's capitalist model, capital is both the objective and the spark that starts it all. It takes money to make money, as the old saying goes.

Capital comes in many forms, but the permanent form of capital is ownership of the enterprise in the form of common stock. That stock is then traded on public exchanges that provide shareholders with liquidity, allowing them to move in and out of specific investments with relative ease.

The first formal stock exchange was set up in Belgium in the early 1500s, but its trade was limited to debt instruments, not stocks. That came later when the Dutch, British, and French government-sponsored monopolies wanted to monetize their trade with East India and Asia.

The first stock exchange in the United States was the Philadelphia Stock Exchange, but the New York Stock Exchange (NYSE), which opened in 1792, just nineteen years after the London Stock Exchange, quickly eclipsed it. As of 2016, the NYSE was home to $18.5 trillion in capital, representing just under 30 percent of the global market for public equities.

Corporations can raise capital on the public stock markets through the initial public offering (IPO), the graduation day, if you will, for most entrepreneurs hoping to cash in on their hard work and ideas. This represents, however, a relatively small slice of the financial pie that changes hands on the public exchanges on a daily basis. In 2016, there were a total of 106 IPOs in the United States, raising just over $20 billion in new capital/personal wealth. It's not peanuts if you are one of those lucky entrepreneurs, but raising fresh capital is no longer one of the primary benefits of public exchanges.

They do, however, support capital formation in another way. Companies can buy other companies using their stock as currency. And if the acquisition is financially or strategically accretive, meaning that the two companies together are worth more than the sum of the two separately, everybody theoretically wins.

It's one of the reasons, although far from the primary one, I would submit, that company executives spend so much time managing their stock price. If investors like your stock, other company executives will too, and the stock becomes a powerful tool for quick growth and the acquisition of either strategic advantage or the preclusion of future competition without the outlay of cash, which young companies in particular normally don't have much of.

Under the laws that govern corporate existence in the United States, the shareholders own the company in which they hold shares. The board of directors, elected by the shareholders, is charged with managing the company on behalf of the shareholders and it, in turn, appoints the professional management of the company that runs the company day to day.

For most of US corporate history, the shareholders, with the few exceptions of families or individuals who had retained effective control of a company that had once been privately held, were largely silent when it came to the company's affairs. As long as they were receiving dividends and the price of the stock trended upward over time, they were largely content to sit back and count their money.

The board of directors, of which I've served on four, was a little more active than shareholders in the management of the company, but not materially so. Board memberships were typically a way for high-profile executives to earn a little extra money, garner some prestige, and in many cases, stay busy in retirement. It was a pretty clubby world, a reality reinforced by the fact that the CEO of the company, usually a hired hand, hand selected the board's members.

In theory the board nominated who was to stand for election, and the shareholders had to vote, but management's recommendations were seldom overruled. And, as a result, it was common for boards to be stacked with known supporters and friends of the CEO. In many cases, CEOs would enter into unofficial reciprocal arrangements with other CEOs, each CEO serving on the board of the other's company, essentially neutralizing their effectiveness in actually contributing to corporate governance.

In the end, management held all the power. It decided what information to share with the board, who would be elected to the board, and what to do with the board's recommendations, if anything. In the end, and I speak from experience, public companies were run very much like private ones. The distinction existed in name only.

In 1927, however, investor Benjamin Graham (1894–1976), known as the father of value investing and mentor to Warren Buffett, used his ownership power to pressure the Northern Pipeline Company to distribute its excess cash to shareholders. It would take another fifty years to fully materialize, but the era of shareholder activism had begun.

Following World War II, with the US economy plowing full steam ahead, stock ownership, which had previously been concentrated in the hands of a small and elite group of Wall Street investors, began to widen, giving birth to a much broader shareholder community looking to actively manage their investments. One particular group of aggressive young investors, who came to be colloquially known as the Proxyteers (The proxy is the legal ballot, if you will, that shareholders use to vote.), began to use their voting rights as shareholders to pressure boards and management. One of the more famous Proxyteers was Robert Young, who used the proxy to become chairman of the New York Central Railroad in the hope of forming a true transcontinental railroad company. Unfortunately, after a long bout with depression, Young committed suicide at his winter home in Palm Beach, Florida.

By the 1980s, the traditional public company stakeholders—the founding families, the employees, and the communities in which the company operated—were increasingly marginalized by active investors more interested in earning a return on their investments than sitting back and waiting for management to reward them with dividends and distributions. Ultimately, men like Carl Icahn and T. Boone Pickens, among other "Masters of the Universe," had management across the corporate spectrum quaking in their boots out of fear that these corporate raiders would gain control of the company and usher them to the street.

In the beginning, with the help of a legion of lawyers and bankers, management fought back. Companies and their boards adopted a variety of poison pills designed to make it irrational for corporate raiders to acquire them uninvited. It worked for a while, but shareholder activism ultimately resurfaced in another form. It was a kinder, gentler form of activism, but no less effective. This second revolution was lead, however, not by bigger-than-life masters of the universe, but by faceless institutions.

The vast majority of US equities are now owned by financial institutions such as hedge funds, retirement funds, and mutual funds managed by companies like Vanguard and Fidelity. Collectively, these institutions now own more than 70 percent of all US stocks. While the theoretical and legal roles of management and the board of directors have not changed, institutional investors and their proxies now control the American corporate landscape.

They don't, however, exercise their power alone. Most institutional investors do not have the inclination or the resources to act prudently on the many proxies they receive from corporations and their boards. As a result, they hire other companies, called proxy advisors, to tell them how to vote their shares. While companies like Institutional Shareholder Services, one of the largest advisory firms, theoretically only advise shareholders, they exercise considerable influence over corporate America.

In essence, we are right back to where we were in the early twentieth century, with a few people, either directly or indirectly, holding sway over the American economy. The players have changed in shape and form, but the end result is effectively the same. A few wealthy individuals have the power to tilt what is supposed to be a free-market economy in their favor. The rich get richer, and the rest of us struggle to get by.

The real losers in this realignment of corporate power have been the employees and the communities in which companies actually conduct their business. Local taxpayers are left with skeletal eyesores, and often reclamation costs, as companies routinely move factories and distribution facilities elsewhere in search of lower costs and higher profits. In the end, corporations have little obligation to these communities that have, in many cases, supported the company for decades through community services, public infrastructure, public education, police and fire protection, and other public services and assets.

No one, however, has lost more than the employees. While US labor law has always favored the company over the employee, as I will discuss in a later chapter, labor relations had long operated under guidelines of a universal if informal labor contract by which companies assumed significant obligation for employee welfare. Give the company an honest day's work, and they will reward you with an honest day's pay and the security of continued employment, health benefits, and a modest retirement.

That informal contract was in full effect when I entered the corporate workforce in the mid-1970s. It never occurred to me or my colleagues that we could lose our jobs in the singular interest of cost reduction or that the company would willingly close the plant or leave the community just because the CEO wanted to live elsewhere or some other community, domestic or foreign, offered attractive financial incentives to move there. It just wasn't done.

Life in the United States, of course, was different in a lot of ways back then. CEOs tended to live in the better neighborhoods in town, but they almost never lived in gated communities, isolated from the people who worked for them. The CEO of the first public company I worked for lived right on Main Street, in a nicer but comparable house to everyone else in the community. And I knew I could walk up to his door and knock at any time, and he would surely listen with sincere interest to whatever I had to say. Most employees today, I venture, don't even know where the CEO actually lives.

There is an old saying, often attributed to Yogi Berra: "In theory there is no difference between practice and theory, but in practice there is." Never was that sentiment more appropriate than in the arena of employee relations. The theory, in theory, hasn't changed, but the practice sure has. And it is this change, the loss of self-imposed obligation of employers to employees, above all else, including the rapid development of new technology, that has turned our society, our culture, our politics, and our economy on its head.

It is the single most important economic reason why the vast majority of employees today feel overwhelming disillusionment and a total lack of control over their lives; it is the single most important reason why drug addiction and suicide continue to rise; it is the single most important reason why 30 percent of our population is on some form of anxiety medication; it is the single most important reason why Congress's approval rating is 10 percent and why we have a mercurial, politically inexperienced billionaire in the White House; it is the single most important reason that the financial elite are getting richer when the average American hasn't seen a wage increase in twenty-five years.

The only question is how long Americans will allow the travesty of zero corporate obligation toward employees to continue. At what point, and I think we might be closer than we think, do we say that enough is enough? At what point do we resurrect the doctrine of personal fairness that I believe is at the heart of what it means to be an American?

In 2014, economist and professor Thomas Piketty wrote the seminal book, *Capital in the Twenty-First Century*. He notes, "Capitalism automatically generates arbitrary and unsustainable inequalities that radically undermine the meritocratic values on which democratic societies are based."

There is a fundamental law of archetypal closed loop modeling that success flows to the successful. It comes from the theoretical concept of leverage. Once one model or participant starts to move ahead, the advantage naturally grows over time.

If a group of people go hiking, for example, some portion of the group will typically get ahead of the rest of the group. At some point, as a result, they stop and wait for the others to catch up. When they start out on the second leg of the journey, however, the gap widens even further. And it widens, stop after stop, until the laggards are well behind.

On the surface, the explanation is simple. The hikers who got ahead initially had a longer chance to rest when they stopped to wait for the others to catch up. And that's true, in part. What causes the group of hikers to spread out further is that the small difference in fitness that manifested itself on the first leg of the journey was leveraged by the rest stops, allowing the nominally more fit hikers to get further and further ahead.

In economic terms, the rich get richer, and they get richer at a faster and faster *relative* pace as time goes on. And now imagine that the rich get hold of the political process and acquire the means to determine who must follow what path to the final destination. They have, in other words, the power to choose the easier path over flat land for themselves, leaving the slower hikers the steep hills and ravines to cross to reach the same destination. No longer are the two groups of hikers even on the same hike.

The process works in reverse as well. Economists at the International Monetary Fund, for example, have found that national income inequality actually reduces the country's overall GDP growth. The rich get a bigger and bigger slice of a pie that is growing slower and slower.

According to a Federal Reserve report released in September 2017, as of 2016 the richest 1 percent of American families now control 39 percent of the country's wealth, while the bottom 90 percent control only 23 percent, down from one-third a quarter of a century ago.

Why does it matter? Isn't this a testament to American opportunity and the reward given to hard work and ingenuity?

It matters for some very important reasons that extend well beyond our individual standard of fairness. The fact is that trickle-down economics doesn't work. Even if the wealthiest households spend every dollar of income, and they obviously don't or they wouldn't be wealthy, their expenditures do not normally drive broad economic progress. It's deleveraged spending. What the wealthy spend goes largely into the pockets of other wealthy people, including the wealthy lawyers, tax advisors, and other personal handlers who cater to them and help them to tilt the playing field even further in their favor.

If you want to help the broader economy, the most productive way to do that is to spend money on goods and services provided by other working people. Setting aside the effect of imports, a dollar spent at Walmart or Target is going to contribute more to the well-being of other working people than a dollar spent at an Apple or Microsoft store.

It's just another form of leverage. And when you understand how the economy really works, rather than how theoretical economists assume it works, the economy is just a giant system of levers and fulcrums. That is why epidemiologists (those who study disease transmission) Richard Wilkonson and Kate Pickett, in their 2009 book, *The Spirit Level*, concluded that national inequality has a greater influence on social welfare than the nation's wealth itself.

It just makes sense.

Ultimately, saying that shareholders own our corporations is like saying the gamblers own the casinos. Like the poker players, we can say, as an alternative, that they own the pot, without owning the cards, the table, and the dealer.

Summary
We must realign the rights of corporate ownership in an effort to enhance collective rather than personal prosperity.

- Shareholders cannot reign supreme. Their rights must better align with their risks and their contribution to collective prosperity.
- Corporations should have extensive and well-documented obligations to their employees and to the communities in which they operate. They should have cradle-to-grave responsibility for the facilities they build and the environment they have impacted.
- The board of directors must have primary responsibility not just to shareholders, but also to all stakeholders. It should be at the board's discretion, moreover, to decide when and how to solicit shareholder opinions or otherwise put matters of corporate governance to a vote.
- Each stakeholder group—employees, creditors, community, shareholders—should have established rights to board representation.

CHAPTER 6

Our Digital World

• • •

The first ultraintelligent machine is the last invention that man need ever make, provided that the machine is docile enough to tell us how to keep it under control.

—IRVING J. GOOD, 1965

GENERAL MOTORS INSTALLED THE FIRST industrial robot in its plant in Ewing Township, New Jersey, in 1961. It was designed by George Devol and built by his company, Unimation. The robot's controls were stored on a magnetic drum, and it was used to move hot die castings and to perform welding on auto bodies, two jobs that are rather unpleasant for humans to perform.

FANUC, a Japanese robotics company, built a prototype of the first "intelligent" robot in 1992. And while programming the controls has always been the limitation in robot development, the company now has robots that essentially program themselves through a technique known as deep reinforcement learning. And the speed at which they do so is already equivalent to an experienced programmer.

Today there are more than 233,000 robots in use in America, more than half of them in just ten Midwestern and Upper Southern states. Michigan has the most, at 28,000, with 12 percent of the nation's total, as many robots as are employed in the entire western half of the country.

Now that robots can program themselves, the historical bottleneck (i.e., control systems) impeding the growth in their application has been effectively eliminated, and their numbers will expand exponentially at a very rapid pace. China has already committed to installing millions, and it won't be long before it feels like robots are everywhere.

Will the robots put us all out of work? That fear, I believe, should be well down the list of our concerns. I am quite confident it won't happen in my own lifetime and is unlikely to happen in that of my daughters. It is unlikely my daughters will make their living welding car bodies, but there will still be a role for human consciousness.

In fact, we—the humans—are the risk, not the robots.

Digital technology, which is at the heart of all things robotic, the Internet, and AI, is ideally suited to pattern recognition. That is how a robot can learn a task. It's also why Alexa and Siri can respond to our questions and why the translation of language is one of AI's most notable successes to date. Language is nothing but a convention of patterns.

So are many other disciplines. Medicine is an excellent example. Doctors don't so much determine what ails you as they eliminate what doesn't. In the end there is an obvious choice, and the treatment has been previously prescribed. Prescription comes from the Latin *praescriptionem*, meaning "a writing before, order, direction." In short, a recognized pattern.

War, unfortunately, is another one. Which is why today's generals study military history. They're searching for patterns, knowing that pattern management, even if it's a pattern of chaos, is ultimately what successful military campaigns are all about.

A lot of what we call science is also a process of pattern recognition. The scientific method is not a body of knowledge, but a process that is largely defined by protocols of pattern recognition. Which is why a lot of science is, according to scientists, a rather tedious affair. That doesn't mean it's boring, because the scientist lives in the contextual world. It does, however, require discipline.

Put war and science together and you have what is, by far, the greatest risk we face from technology and AI, the latter being the brain that drives the technology. It has already revolutionized modern warfare. Drone pilots sitting in Florida today routinely direct and execute violence on the other side of the world in real-time.

And because the technology of war is built on pattern recognition and digital communication organized into global networks, it will, like water, seek its own level. We can slow it down but we can't stop it. The technology of death, in other words, will be distributed across the globe in something very close to real time.

Which is precisely why computer hacking is now one of our most immediate and far-reaching political, technological, and economic threats. It is, statistically speaking, absurd and naïve to believe that our most feared enemies, however we may define them, don't already have whatever secrets of death we may have sitting in top secret military installations somewhere most of us have never heard of.

It is logically irrational to believe that North Korea, for example, has developed its ability to wage nuclear war on its own. It's a nation of 22 million people of modest education. Statistically speaking, it's highly unlikely, no matter how motivated they may be.

The technology of death is, by far, the biggest conundrum we face in the twenty-first century. If we develop it, we are, as a practical matter, developing it for the use of the world. And if we don't, someone else might, and while that technology will ultimately seek global equilibrium, it will only take the briefest of head starts to destroy the planet.

While we may ultimately fail, what choice do we realistically have but to direct the development of AI going forward? As Elon Musk and Stephen Hawking, among many other knowledgeable people, have urged us to do, we need to reach some consensus on the regulation of AI, or at least the regulation of the development of AI. We can't just leave it to free-market forces and the invisible hand of self-interest. The stakes are too high and the outcome effectively certain.

We must further recognize, of course, that not all death and destruction is quite so direct and obvious as a rogue state's possession of nuclear weapons. There were, as one example, more than forty thousand deaths on US roads in 2016, according to the National Safety Council.

And, of course, we are on the verge of driverless cars. Many prototypes are already being tested on actual city streets. And if experts are right, driverless cars should reduce traffic fatalities by 70 percent or more. But what about the other 30 percent? Who dies?

Imagine you are driving on a mountain road with a rock face on the left and a one-hundred-foot drop on the right. You come around a bend and see a large boulder blocking your lane, and there is virtually no chance to stop in time. What to do? Now assume that there is a school bus full of children, or convicts, or a single passenger who happens to be a US senator, coming the other way in the unblocked lane and will reach the boulder at the same time you do.

What to do? The driverless car cannot and will not make up its own mind. And there will not be time for the human to take control. The car's response, if any, and no response is the same as a willful response, will have to be programmed in ahead of time.

So, do we want to put that decision in the hands of the people who program our driverless cars? Germany has already said no and has issued guidelines for companies to follow in those circumstances. In the United States, however, no such official guidelines exist.

The libertarians that dominate technology, of course, will trivialize the issue as irrelevant, noting that there are no such morality questions on the typical test to obtain a driver's license. Why, then, should the makers of self-driving cars be burdened with such a requirement?

The distinction, of course, is obvious. A person who makes a moral decision while driving is making an isolated decision. If they choose an unpopular option, the loss is limited to that one accident.

Not so with self-driving cars, however, assuming that every driver won't be programming his or her own vehicle. It is safe to say that only a handful of companies and their engineers will provide such software. How they decide to address the moral choice, therefore, will have far-reaching impact.

In the end, moreover, taking a position is unavoidable. If the developers of driverless technology don't address it upfront, the personal injury lawyers will force them to face it as soon as there is a fatal accident. And the solution, we can assume, will be a lot more expensive and a lot less organized.

Unfortunately, the need to manage the development of the technology of death is only the most obvious need and perhaps the easiest to address. There are far less obvious threats that are just now starting to be recognized and understood.

Because digital technology turns on pattern recognition, the intelligence of digital technology resides in the algorithm. It is the algorithm that is ultimately at the heart of all digital technology, from the Internet to the apps we use on our smartphones.

An algorithm is a recursive mathematical procedure used to "solve" problems. What an algorithm really does, however, is to provide an answer, which may approximate a solution, but not necessarily. Amazon uses algorithms to suggest which books you might be interested in. Google uses them to determine how to respond to your search query. And Facebook uses them to recommend new friends and to build your news feed.

The important thing to remember is that an algorithm is a computational process; it is not a computation, like 2+2=4. It provides an answer, not a solution. This is why searching is often a recurring process, and media sites like Facebook and MSN may sometimes display information that seems just a bit out of place.

A process is not subject to the same singularity and universality that a calculation is. An algorithm is a series of digital computations that behave like a calculation but are far more subjective. The decisional computations built into the algorithm collectively answer a question, but don't actually compute it.

This reality is seldom discussed but has two far-reaching implications. The first is that the algorithms used by companies like Facebook evolve in much the same way a mason builds a brick wall. (The coders are the masons.) At some point the algorithm will become so complex that the people coding the algorithm will themselves not really know how it works. They know the algorithm yields acceptable answers, but they're not sure why.

Some believe the tech giants have already reached this level of complexity. Cornell University computer scientist Jon Kleinberg, educated at MIT and a recipient of the Nevanlinna Prize, wrote, "We have, perhaps for the first time ever, built machines we do not understand." And they're built on a foundation of algorithms.

Perhaps the bigger issue, however, is that algorithms are discrete and finite. By definition they must, therefore, be biased to the same extent human thought is. (And mathematical calculation cannot be.) As Franklin Foer, the author of *World Without Mind*, puts it, "The problem is that when we outsource thinking to machines, we are really outsourcing thinking to the organizations that run the machines." All thanks to the magic of algorithms.

That matters because people are biased, in part because we, too, use a form of algorithm to think. Psychologists call it precognitive conclusion. Our brains only process a fraction of the data our senses make available simply as a matter of efficiency. Without precognitive conclusion, we'd never get out of bed in the morning.

In the case of people, those internal algorithms are based on our prior experience and whatever values we've acquired or established out of that experience. From any philosophical perspective, absolute objectivity is an unattainable ideal. There just isn't time, even if we did have the sensory and processing power, which we don't, and, by definition, never will. If such a person or machine did exist, he, she, or it would be God.

Facebook and Google face the same limitation. The recent public horror over "fake news" highlights the catch-22 we face. Executives in Silicon Valley surely recognize the bias inherent in algorithms. The very fact that it exists is undoubtedly proof of their awareness. However, recognizing the bias inherent in algorithms and being of a libertarian mind-set, in which individual freedoms reign supreme, they have consciously avoided developing the algorithms that could detect false news in the realization that those algorithms would, by definition, overshoot the mark and result in the kind of censorship that we so abhor as a liberal democracy.

This reality, moreover, is itself reinforced by the algorithmic structure on which the Internet exists. When applied to communication, algorithms naturally recreate reinforcing loops. That's precisely why they exist in the first place.

Online news feeds and social communities, as a result, will, by definition, drive division and extremism. It is the very same reason that, as discussed in the last chapter, success flows to the successful.

It's all about leverage and its impact on the performance of the closed loop. It's all about the lead hiker getting further and further ahead based on his or her performance in the first mile.

More algorithms are obviously not the answer, which, I suspect, is what is keeping the executives at Facebook and Google up at night. In small doses, algorithms are extremely helpful. In large doses, they are the ultimate tools of tyranny.

In his popular and very worthy book *WTF?: What's the Future and Why It's Up to Us*, Silicon Valley insider and expert Tim O'Reilly notes: "Algorithmically derived knowledge is a new source of asymmetric market power." And, of course, market power is universal. The only distinction among us is what we're selling.

Which is precisely why the biggest threat to our future politically, socially, and commercially is the commercialization of the Internet. A commercial market of any form, be it politics or business, is a closed-loop system that is, by definition, susceptible to the distortion of leverage.

Facebook now has more than two billion users. Why? Is it really better than its rivals? Maybe. Once Facebook and its fellow hikers in social media set out on their journey, for whatever reason, Facebook took the lead. And once they had separated from the pack, of course, they leveraged that lead by virtue of the fact that everyone naturally wants to join whatever social network that their friends and family are on. Within certain limits, in other words, Facebook's success has had nothing to do with Facebook itself.

This, of course, leads to several important questions. For starters, is it reasonable for Mark Zuckerberg, however bright and driven he might be, to be worth, according to Forbes, more than $72 billion as of July 2017? I mean no disrespect for the individual. I'm sure he's brilliant and possibly engaging. But, come on; is any one person really worth that much? (Of course, we must ask the same question of Jeff Bezos, Bill Gates, and Warren Buffett, as well as every one of the more than five hundred billionaires there are in the United States today.)

We must remember, moreover, that the economy is itself a functional loop of levers and fulcrums. Wealth begets wealth, as Warren Buffett has demonstrated so conclusively. (Again, taking nothing away from the individual.) Left unchecked, just as the second law of thermodynamics teaches us, the imbalance will continue to grow and grow.

Politically, we must recognize the distortive weakness of the news media. We can't ever eradicate that bias as it is inherent to the market for information itself. We can, however, limit its impact by limiting the scale of the content providers. We should tremble at the very thought of any one news loop having two billion subscribers. If we don't wish to limit its size, we should, at the very least, limit the scope of the information it feeds us.

Media is media, and we should both limit its concentration and define it for what it is. The idea that Facebook is not a media company but a digital platform, as its executives have repeatedly argued, is patently absurd. It's like saying that McDonald's is merely a delivery platform for fast food and should not be accountable for the ingredients in its burgers.

There is, however, another element to this whole debate that I believe is more urgent and of even greater importance. That is access to education.

In the technological world of the future, education will be more important than ever. Not because technology will require specialized knowledge to use it. Technology will be well qualified to dumb itself down to the level of a monkey or a dog.

And isn't that how all fictional dystopias are ultimately created? Orwell and others intuitively understood the impact of levers and fulcrums on the market of knowledge and that the leverage can be applied in both directions—to liberate *and* to repress. Knowledge is the great equalizer. It is, ultimately, the *only* equalizer.

We need broad-based knowledge, in other words, not to learn how to use technology or even to develop it. We need to learn so that we continue to recognize it for what it is.

Which is why, I believe, we should teach philosophy with the same energy with which we teach mathematics. We should teach art and art history with the same dedication we give to science. We should teach communication with the same intensity we teach coding and programming.

This is also, I believe, why education should be free and accessible to all. The commercialization of education, which we are already well along the path of, will create an educated elite that will inevitably, consciously or not, use its leverage to further extend the divide. The end result is, in turn, an inevitable dystopia. (Until, of course, someone in the uneducated masses figures out just enough to master the technology of death and kills us all.)

On the social front, unfortunately, free education will probably be of little value in minimizing the harmful effects of digital social media and the entropic impact it has on social community. The risk, in this case, has less to do with commercialization than it does access.

Sean Parker, of Napster fame and an early investor in Facebook who went on to become the company's first president, now laments the work they did at Facebook, recognizing that they were "exploiting a vulnerability in human psychology."

Chamath Palihapitiya, a former Facebook vice president responsible for user growth, likewise recently told an audience at the Stanford Graduate School of Business that he feels "tremendous guilt" for his hand in creating "tools that are ripping apart the social fabric of how society works." He adds: "No civil discourse, no cooperation; misinformation, mistruth…this is not about Russian ads. This is a global problem."

And so it is.

Summary

We must recognize the inherent susceptibility to bias and its leverage in all closed systems. There are great risks in commercializing our society and the information flow that defines it and its potential.

We must:

- Prevent digital monopolies with the same diligence as we prevent other commercial monopolies.
- Make education free and accessible to all.
- Redefine the educational agenda to balance the STEM subjects and the liberal arts.
- Reform the rules and regulations surrounding personal wealth.
- Manage social media companies in the same way we manage other media companies. At the very least, maintain a clear distinction between news and social media.
- Develop consensus rules and conventions to guide the development of artificial intelligence, ensuring that, at the very least, it cannot be used to develop the technology of destruction.

PART II
Social
• • •

CHAPTER 7

Wages

• • •

The rich will do anything for the poor but get off their backs.

—KARL MARX (1818–1883)

FOR A PERIOD OF TIME in the 1990s, I was the CEO of Lionel Trains, the iconic toy train company. I was hired by the private equity firm started by Martin Davis, the former CEO of Paramount and one of the lead players in the saga of RJR chronicled by the hit book *Barbarians at the Gate*. Neil Young, the rock legend and a technology enthusiast, was also an investment partner in the company.

Martin ultimately fired me, but if you know anything about Martin's career, you know I was in very good company. His reputation for being a tough boss, in every sense of the word, was legendary. And he could be crotchety, for sure. I don't think I ever dined publicly with him when he didn't send something back to the kitchen. Nonetheless, he was, behind the gruff exterior, one of the most humble, principled, and generous people I've ever met.

I could also tell stories about the time I spent with Neil, but I won't. I did, however, very much enjoy our time together, and his long-time agent, Eliot Roberts, taught me a great deal about people and business. He is a master at both. And I will say that from what I saw, Neil's legions of fans would not be the least bit disappointed in the man he is when out of the public eye. He is the very definition of authentic.

I enjoyed my time at Lionel immensely, despite the ending, but I did learn not to advertise the fact that I worked for the company when introduced to strangers. While doing paperwork on airplanes, I would make sure to cover up the Lionel name or logo if it appeared on any of the material I was working on.

My reason for doing so was quite simple. As soon as someone discovered that I worked for Lionel, they would say, "You know, I have an old Lionel train set up in the attic that my father had when he was a kid. What do you suppose it might be worth?" To which I would always reply, "Whatever someone is willing to pay you for it."

And that, of course, is the truth about the financial worth of anything, including our labor. While economists assume that wages and nonwage income are defined by efficient market forces, nothing could be further from the truth.

In 1978, Ben Cohen and Jerry Greenfield, a couple of New York–born hippies then living in Vermont, started Ben & Jerry's Homemade Holdings, Inc., the iconic premium ice-cream manufacturer known for quirky flavors like Cherry Garcia and Phish Food. They were also known, however, for making a promise to employees that the highest-paid executive would never be paid more than five times the amount paid to the lowest-level worker in the company. And for sixteen years they made good on the promise.

The company was sold to Unilever in 2000, so we don't know what the head of the ice-cream division makes today. The CEO of Unilever, however, in 2014, made just over $9 million, and it's highly unlikely that the lowest paid employee in Unilever is making anything close to $1.8 million per year.

Ben & Jerry's was not the first company to abide by such a policy. My own first employer, Oneida Ltd., the corporate afterlife of the Oneida Community, followed a similar protocol well into the latter half of the twentieth century, when the company went public on the NYSE.

If there are any such companies around today, they're well hidden, and they certainly don't have a Wall Street, Menlo Park, or Mountain View mailing address. The top executives of corporate America today earn, on average, 373 times the income of the company's average worker. That's almost a tenfold increase in *multiple* in less than forty years.

The story of how that happened is a classic tale of unintended consequence. And in this case, there were two storylines that contributed to what is one of the greatest absurdities in American history and perhaps the lynchpin holding together an increasingly fragile social peace in the United States today.

The first storyline was the one referenced in an earlier chapter. With the rising supremacy of the shareholder and the increasingly aggressive tactics they were willing to pursue to increase the return on their investment, activist investors put increasing pressure on the compensation committees of the boards of directors to tie executive compensation to corporate performance. And, of course, the only performance they really cared about was the price of the stock. They wanted their CEOs to think like stockholders.

The second storyline was the popular backlash against the rapid rise in executive compensation in the late '80s and early '90s. In 1993, as a result, Bill Clinton, having been elected president on the campaign promise of "Putting People First," enacted legislation to cap the tax deduction that companies could take on executive compensation as a way to prevent any taxpayer subsidy of egregious salaries and bonuses. The legislation that finally passed, however, included a "performance" loophole bigger than Wall Street itself. (Robert Reich, Clinton's labor secretary, I must say, lobbied against the blatant gutting of the bill.)

The net result of both storylines was to accelerate the rate of increase in executive compensation by essentially making those same executives among the primary beneficiaries of run ups in the companies' stock price, regardless of the companies' overall financial performance or social contribution.

Following the financial crisis of 2008, a collapse directly triggered by greedy bankers who abandoned any sense of fiduciary responsibility, the US Treasury was forced to inject $700 billion of taxpayer money into the financial markets, more than $2,000 for every man, woman, and child in America, to prevent a financial Armageddon that would have quickly spread around the globe.

In the years following the taxpayer bailout, however, the twenty leading US banks paid out more than $800 million in "performance" bonuses to their executives, *before* the price of the bank's stock had even returned to precrash levels. According to the Joint Committee on Taxation, moreover, the taxpayers lose $5 billion per year in tax revenues because executive compensation based on "performance" remains fully deductible.

According to the Associated Press, American CEOs received a median compensation of $11.5 million in 2016. The top five were awarded $278 million for their troubles. That's equivalent to the total annual income of 4,700 US households earning the United States median income—for just five executives who were the equivalent of hired employees.

If you still believe that the United States employment markets are efficient in any reasonable economic sense, ask yourself this: Looking back on the #MeToo campaign of 2017, why did so many women wait so long to tell their stories of sexual abuse and mistreatment at the hands of powerful men? There are undoubtedly a lot of reasons, most of which I am not qualified to address. One reason, however, seems obvious, and anyone who has ever held a job in America can relate to it.

The #MeToo campaign was, first and foremost, about sexual abuse and gender discrimination. It was as well, however, a story about the abuse of organizational power. Whether stated or implied, whether direct or by proxy, every woman was confronted with the potential backlash of a powerful man whom she feared could destroy or damage her career.

In a truly efficient labor market, of course, you always have the option of leaving and finding work elsewhere, away from the predator. In an efficient world in which you're paid what you're worth, switching employers should be relatively straightforward and should not impact your income in any material way.

I would hazard to guess, however, that for the vast majority of Americans over the age of forty-five who are not stuck at the lowest rungs of the employment ladder, such mobility simply does not exist. Most people who have known even modest career success are stuck where they are and they know it. Which is why they put up with jobs that bring them little or no satisfaction, and, in many cases, a whole lot of stress and aggravation—even abuse.

Unfortunately, left unchecked, the problem will get worse—far worse—before it gets better. Money, in a commercialized world, is power. And power responds to the same laws of the universe as everything else. In a self-reinforcing loop of levers and fulcrums, power begets power, and the differential expands over time.

The biggest challenge organizational leaders face is getting access to accurate and complete information. While they may have plenty of electronic dashboards displaying key metrics in a colorful array of red, yellow, and green, it is context that they really need to make informed decisions. And the context is seldom obvious in the array of dashboards and spreadsheets. Almost always, context is provided by people and acquired through experience.

The practical effect is that the performance that really matters, at least in terms of employee performance evaluations, is largely communicated up the chain of command and is, quite naturally, filtered at every level of the organization to reflect most positively on the individual transferring the knowledge to the next level. By the time it gets to the key decision-makers at the top, history has been largely rewritten.

Management by walking around (MBWA), a term coined by business guru Tom Peters, can help, but only if it's consistent and the executive has demonstrated that he or she will use the information gained responsibly. Relatively few executives, it's sad to say, pass the test.

But let's go back to our simple example of the group of hikers setting out on a journey. And let's assume that the leader of our group of hikers has enough greater skill and fitness that the group recognizes him or her, let's say her this time, as the leader who shall hike independently at the head of the line, unrestrained by the pace of the hikers behind her. At the first rest stop, our leader stops and waits for the last hiker to catch up and then, as a unified group, they set out again. And at the second rest stop, of course, all things being equal, our leader is even further ahead than she was at the first rest stop as she has leveraged her once modest superiority in hiking by the additional rest she enjoyed at the first rest stop.

As the day wears on, our intrepid leader gets further and further ahead at each rest stop. At the next rest stop, however, she is given a new pair of hiking boots that are lighter and more comfortable than the boots issued to everyone at the beginning of the hike. It's a reward for her great performance, so only she is given the better boots. There are no participation trophies in this hiking club.

At the next rest stop, the group reassembles yet again, and when it sets out, our leader, now far more rested than any other hiker and enjoying the spring of her new boots, gets well ahead of the rest of the group until she is, in fact, hiking in a completely different weather system than the hikers at the end of the line. And let's assume that her weather is sunny and dry and the temperature could not be more pleasant. The laggards, however, are forced to push on in a driving, cold rain on the verge of freezing.

You get the picture.

What's the solution? There are actually many possible solutions. But they all have one thing in common. Each of them involves a fundamental shift in paradigm. Instead of viewing our hikers as a group of independent individuals, each moving at his or her own pace and each relying on his or her individual and innate abilities and motivation and rewarded accordingly, they are viewed as a single, collective entity whose progress is measured solely by the performance of the collective.

The leader, of course, is not happy. She wants to be recognized for her individual performance. Why should she be dragged down by the hikers who don't work as hard as she does? This is America; it's not fair. (And she really likes the new boots she got for her performance.)

Of course it's not. And that's exactly what I believed for most of my working career. I, like almost every other executive of my generation, was a disciple of rugged individualism. America is the land of opportunity; you get what you deserve.

Not.

Why is our lead hiker better than the rest? Perhaps her mother was a good hiker, and she inherited her genetic makeup. Perhaps she grew up in a wealthy household and had access to better, healthier food. Perhaps she was fortunate enough not to live in one of Asia's more polluted cities, where people wear facemasks to protect them from filthy air. Perhaps she got to attend a school with a very good hiking program because her father went there and was a legacy, virtually guaranteeing her acceptance.

The one thing that all of these advantages have in common is that they had nothing to do with her, the person. All were advantages that accrued to her by fate. And fate, of course, is not fair.

But let's assume she does, in fact, train harder than any of the other hikers. Fair enough; that's personal. And she deserves recognition for that individual effort. After several years of slogging away on the trail, however, enjoying her distinction as the best hiker, she begins to realize that arriving at the next rest area first brings her little sense of accomplishment or satisfaction. She's a social person, after all, and most enjoys the times when the entire team is together.

And she's getting older. She can no longer maintain the pace she once did. The younger hikers are starting to pass her and leverage their own advantage of youth.

So, here's the lesson to be learned. Yes, there are differences in individual effort and performance, but it is virtually impossible to isolate and measure those differences. You will spend far more time and effort trying to sort it all out.

Pay for performance is not a new concept. It's been around for centuries. While I was attending college, I spent a couple of summers working in a large factory that employed a piecework system of compensation. You were, in the most literal sense, paid for the pieces you produced. And performance was strictly measured on a personal level. To each, his own.

Management, however, monitored each employee's earnings very carefully. In some cases, workers cheated—surprise, surprise.

They took finished pieces out of someone else's box and put them in their own. Or they bribed the stock handlers with money, or, in fact, sexual favors (I kid you not.), to bring them the jobs with the loosest standards.

In other cases, employees simply got more efficient with practice, as the learning curve, first identified by German psychologist Hermann Ebbinghaus (1850–1909) virtually guarantees. Or there was some alteration in the product itself or in the way previous steps in the process were performed that ultimately made this step easier.

Either way, if wages (like Google's algorithms) started behaving unexpectedly, management sent out the industrial engineers to perform time and motion studies to reset the rate. But guess what? Every operator knew who the industrial engineers were, and when they showed up, stopwatch and clipboard in hand, a not-so-strange thing happened. Productivity dropped like a rock. Trust me, you won't find that kind of acting in Hollywood or on a New York stage.

Ultimately, management decided, like many other managements, that the system was both giving the workers inappropriate incentives and wasn't worth the significant overhead cost it required to maintain it and to arbitrate the results, which employees, naturally enough, were constantly challenging. So the company did away with it.

What we have today in executive compensation is piecework on steroids. And we're not getting much benefit from the system. We're throwing a lot of money against the wall and little of it actually sticks. Remember, the average tenure of a CEO today is only three years.

But won't companies have to hire a lot more people to do the same work if they don't pay for performance?

I'll let you in on another dirty little corporate secret. When I landed my first corporate job in 1977, I earned a salary of $11,200 per year, and I thought I had died and gone to heaven. By the time I finally retired, my income was a multiple of that—a big multiple.

At the height of my career, however, I was putting in a fraction of the effort I did during those early years. I fulfilled my obligation, mind you, and, on the surface, it certainly appeared I was putting in a lot of hours and spending a lot of time on airplanes. And I worked a lot more efficiently, given my additional experience. But my effort, of and by itself, had little to do with my salary. It had everything to do with my future and what I perceived was the opportunity to win, however that was defined.

Do you think that the partners at most professional firms are the hardest workers in the firm? They're not. It's the people hoping to become partners that are burning the candle at both ends. And will they turn down the flame if being a partner doesn't mean having a beach house in the Hamptons? No. They do it for the recognition, not the reward.

No one has ever gotten greater personal fulfillment by owning more property. No one ever lay on his or her deathbed and asked the nurse, "Please bring me my stuff." It's a universal and timeless truth that fame and fortune will not bring you happiness and a sense of belonging. The truth is obvious if you just look around.

What to do? If personal incentives aren't really working and are inherently flawed anyway, what is the alternative? Pay everyone the same amount? Reward participation and forget about performance?

Absolutely not. Homogeneity is seldom the answer where motivational trade-offs are involved. We shouldn't treat these choices as digital. We should, however, recognize the real motivation (i.e., recognition) and seek to establish some level of reasonable balance.

Robert Townsend (1920–1998) was a corporate legend best known for his success as the CEO of Avis during its "We Try Harder" era. One of his principles of management was that the compensation differential between any two levels in an organizational hierarchy should never be greater than 30 percent. All things considered, I think it's a pretty good rule of thumb. In a ten-tier hierarchy, that means the top dog is making a little more than ten times the lowest-paid employees. It's twice as generous as Ben and Jerry were, but well below the current reality. Just think how much more money the shareholders will make.

If you're still not convinced, consider the situation in Japan. Japanese culture is collectivist in perspective. If you want to run a sales contest among your employees in Japan, you would never run the kind of individualized contest that would be run in the United States. Sales would be likely to go down. Instead, you run a contest pitting one office against another. You motivate the teams, not the individuals.

And no one who has done business in Japan would ever argue that the Japanese don't work hard. The Japanese even have a name for it—*karoshi*—meaning death from overwork. The government is now stepping in and coercing companies to give its employees a break.

In the end, I add my voice to the growing chorus of people in favor of a universal wage, sometimes called a living wage. It won't be perfect. Few things ever are. But it is, I now believe, the only practical alternative. And the justification is pretty simple:

- Over the course of history, the ultimate social safety net was nature. When all else failed, people could live off of Mother Earth. But that option is no longer available. We have commercialized society to the extent that living without money is no longer an option.
- If we have no obligation to take care of those not in a position to help themselves, we really have no right to call ourselves

a civilized society. This isn't about religion or God. This is about compassion.
- The inequity of wealth and income will eventually cripple the economy. Trickle-down is a myth. What drives the economy is working people spending money on the products and services provided by other working people.

Due to our past success in economic growth and technological advancement, we have reached the tipping point on the individual/collective continuum. It is no longer practical or advisable to continue to measure and reward individual contribution in the ways we have historically. There are too many of us, and the world we live in, largely due to technology, is too integrated to sort out its individual components and their contribution.

Summary

We must realign our standards of income and wealth.

- Corporate bylaws should establish strict and reasonable standards to limit compensatory differentials in the workplace.
- Tax laws should be rewritten to preclude taxpayer funding of irresponsible executive compensation schemes.
- Compensatory differentials among employees should be reasonable and attributable to only those variables (e.g., years of service), which can be easily measured and understood.
- We should develop and implement the foundations of a living-wage system that guarantees all households the ability to sustain a modest, self-reliant, and sustainable lifestyle.

CHAPTER 8

Media

• • •

Whoever controls the media, controls the mind.

—Jim Morrison (1943–1971)

Thomas Jefferson spoke for the Founding Fathers when he noted, "Our liberty depends on the freedom of the press, and that cannot be limited without being lost." It's a sentiment that has been repeated again and again throughout American history. And, of course, it's true. Or is it?

Either way, the press is an anachronism. The word itself is a symbolic reference to Gutenberg's fifteenth-century adaptation of the screw press for the automation of the preparation of written communication. It was, at the time, the only method for cheap, efficient, consistent, and far-reaching communication.

At the heart of all communication, however, is information. And it is information that is ultimately at the center of all power. Without information, even physical power is easily thwarted or neutralized.

Information, however, as is language, is a convention. It can be true, and it can be false. And it can be true and false in isolation. Information is not truth any more than knowledge is wisdom.

But a funny thing happened on the way to our current world. The price of communication dropped to zero. That drop in cost, however, only exists if we can assume the veracity of the information provided. And we can't. I think of the problem as science meets the Internet.

The scientific method is not a body of knowledge. It is neither more nor less than a methodology for interpreting reality. And it is a powerful and informative methodology, to be sure. It is not, however, without potential flaws, as can be said of every human convention for the simple reason that no convention can be just about everything given the ultimate duality of the universe. True and false, fact and fiction, even good and evil, are all relative notions. They can only be defined in context.

English biochemist, author, and researcher Rupert Sheldrake refers to the problem as "the science delusion." He gave an informative TED Talk on the topic that was unfortunately censored from the TED website due to the protestations of other scientists who believed his was a voice that should be silenced. It's back up now, but with a trigger warning, one of those irrational modern compromises that use the conventionality of language to discredit reality in the name of reality.

In Sheldrake's case, the misleading characterization is based on his assertion of ten presumed scientific dogmas that are themselves not authoritative in any scientific way. These include the underlying assumption that the universe is ultimately mechanical and that the discrete variables that can be measured can ever be all-inclusive. Neither assumption is valid except in the closed-loop logic of the presumed science itself.

If science has taught us anything, it is the degree to which the universe is an integrated lattice of related, dependent systems. Nothing happens in isolation, which the Buddhists, of course, have been saying for millennia. Environmental degradation is but one example of the way in which one sphere of human activity impacts every other. Moving production from the United States to a low wage country doesn't just reduce the cost of that product to the United States consumer; it puts downward pressure on all US wages.

In the end, science is theoretically objective. In practice, however, it may not be. It is often difficult to distinguish between true cause and coincidence. Any statistical relationship may be happenstance, and even a causal variable may be a simple proxy for another more definitive causal variable.

Marcis Angell, a former editor of the *New England Journal of Medicine*, has this to say: "It is simply no longer possible to believe much of the clinical research that is published." Stanford researcher John Ioannidis agrees. He has published a paper entitled "Why Most Published Research is False," noting that most research is better at cataloguing the prevailing bias among scientists than discovering new scientific truths.

The proof is in the pudding. The scientific method is based on replicability. Cause and effect, science holds, is fixed by the laws of nature. In one recent study, however, researchers attempted to replicate the results of one hundred published psychology studies and failed to do so in 65 percent of the cases. It's not a rare finding.

The language of science, unfortunately, has been appropriated not just by charlatans and snake oil salesman, but by those we trust to give us honest and unbiased information. How often do you find articles on your online news feed, for example, under the heading, "This is what science says about _____."

The implication, of course, is that it must be true. In reality, however, science has little to say about what is and is not true, any more than the American criminal justice system is ultimately driven by a quest for justice. Science is merely a methodology for getting as close to the truth as we know how. Whether or not it is true or not will inevitably remain open to debate. And, of course, the truth, like everything else, always exists within a defined context within which the truth was determined and is ultimately applied.

For this and other reasons, data, on balance, is no more precise than language. It can have vastly different meaning when used in different contexts.

If, for example, I were to reveal that I weigh 175 pounds, or 79.4 kilograms, you might shrug and think, "That's pretty typical." If I subsequently reveal that I am six feet, six inches in height, or about 198 centimeters, however, you would probably conclude that I must be quite thin. Conversely, if I were to suggest that I am only five feet in height, or 152 centimeters, you might conclude that I must be rather stocky in appearance.

While your description of me may have changed rather dramatically, in other words, the original and core truth—that I weigh 175 pounds—was accurately reported and remains constant. In the end, our ability to measure something, which is at the heart of all science, is no more precise than our ability to describe it. Data, even if scientifically measured, has no meaning outside of its context.

That context, moreover, is not discrete and finite. It is continuous and infinite. It does not have dimension. It can only be measured in areas that extend in a near infinite number of directions all at once.

Imagine you are looking at your house on Google Earth. You can zoom in and out on any specific part of the image. And, in theory, you can back up all the way to the other side of the universe, or you can zoom in on a single atom or subatomic particle in the floor of your basement. The house you are looking at, however, never actually changes. It remains "true." Only the perspective has changed as you have viewed the image in all of its varying contexts.

In the extreme, you can begin to see why some philosophers have concluded that reality is an illusion and that nothing is really knowable or tangible. We know what we see, but do we understand the larger context? It's all one giant relational enigma.

I don't take the logic that far, however, because I think it's essentially illogical to reason that which really doesn't matter in the end. I do, however, take it far enough to recognize that science, at its core, deals in probabilities, not truths. All science, in other words, is provisional. It's true only until it's not—without ever really changing.

Genetic psychologists, for example, do not now believe that genetics defines psychology in any absolute sense, as many scientists once speculated. They assign different probabilities to heritable and environmental factors based on research data. In his 2017 book, *Machiavellianism*, for example, researcher Támas Bereczkei notes that "only 31 percent of the individual variance on the Mach scales [a measure of Machiavellian tendencies] can be explained by genetic factors while the remaining 69 percent is due to environmental influence."

Now throw technology into the equation. At the top of the list of technological developments that have impacted our world, the Internet stands alone. But even it is only one form of a much larger development that we can think of as digital technology—the many forms of technology built on the back of the microchip.

All digital technology, of course, is, well, digital. We think of it as sequences of 0's and 1's, but that's just the symbolism for the real building block of digital technology—a simple electrical switch that is either on or off. By stringing them together and manipulating them to our will, we, in both a figurative and literal sense, simulate the human brain, without, for now, human consciousness, which may or may not be digital.

Digital technology, like science, is discrete. And, like much of science, most of its most complicated and impressive work is measured in probabilities, not absolutes. Computers are very good at performing mathematical calculations because they are, themselves, digital in nature. And they can perform such calculations incredibly fast.

A calculation, of course, is a pattern. The rules of mathematics are absolute, discrete, and knowable at a digital level. So, when we turn that computing power around, computers are very good at finding patterns in discrete data.

If you look at the areas in which computers have had the greatest impact to date, you will note that they all involve patterns. Music is defined by patterns of notes and sounds. Books are merely expressive patterns of words and letters. A digital picture is just a pattern of discrete points of light and color. A video is just a pattern that changes over time. Even language is ultimately a human convention of both audible and written patterns. Which is why computers are very good at translation and artificial intelligence (AI) may soon make it possible for two people to carry on an active conversation in two different languages.

Pattern recognition, however, is not thought, except at the most fundamental and crudest level. Or it is, if you can visualize and work with patterns in infinite dimensions. Which I can't, and it's unlikely computers will ever be able to, since infinity is only definable in relative theoretical terms.

But people, as clever as we can be, have found a way around the problem. It's called an *algorithm*, which we visited at some length back in chapter 5.

Muhammad ibn Musa al-Khwarizmi was a ninth-century mathematician born near the Aral Sea, who later moved to Baghdad. He wrote a treatise on the use of Arabic numerals for mathematical computation, a concept that came to be known as algorism, derived from the English translation of the mathematician's name. Algorism morphed into algorithm and is now synonymous with modern computing.

An algorithm, as we discussed, is a recursive mathematical procedure that both finds and uses patterns in data to find solutions that we hope are very close to rational answers. When done well, it is a process that looks a lot like thought, although that is actually an illusion. (But so, perhaps, is reality.)

And if computers can think, even in a very crude sense, they can also learn. By processing test data over and over again at inhuman speed, algorithmic systems can now fine-tune the computations in search of increasingly relevant answers. Computers are now so fast and powerful that they can, in fact, find patterns that humans have previously overlooked.

In 2016, an artificially intelligent machine, for the first time, beat one of the world's best Go players, Lee Sedol. (Machines had been beating the world's best chess players for a decade by then.) The AI system, known as AlphaGo, was designed by researchers at DeepMind, a London AI lab now owned by Google. What was most amazing about the victory, however, was that in game two of the best-of-five series, the machine made a move that no experienced human Go player would ever consciously make. Sedol was so perplexed by the move that he had to leave the room to work out his response.

AlphaGo won the match in only three games, but in game four, Sedol himself, with nothing left to lose, tried an unexpected move that became known as "God's Touch." The machine, in all of its learning, had never considered the move, and its reaction was disastrous. Sedol won the game, and he did so, for the first time, by simply pursuing a pattern that he would not normally pursue and the machine did not recognize.

But of course there is a duality. While machines can use algorithms to exploit patterns, they are simultaneously vulnerable to them. They may be wrong, but, worse than that, they may, in fact, be evil. Or at least behave in an evil way.

Consider the experience of Carole Cadwalladr, a writer for *The Guardian*. One Sunday night she sat down at her computer and typed "Are Jews" into Google. And the Google algorithms offered a variety of options based on previous patterns. One option Google offered was, "Are Jews evil?"

When she clicked on the suggestion, of course, Google immediately filled her screen with articles and links that concluded that Jews are, in fact, evil. The article listed first was entitled "Top 10 Major Reasons Why People Hate Jews." You can fill in the rest on your own.

It is a good example of the dark side to patterns and the algorithm's ability to exploit or lever them. Sexism, racism, and misogyny are, in the end, all precoded reactions to patterns. They are patterned reactions to other patterns.

It's another variation of the issue of context. It would be ludicrous to suggest that anyone at Google hates Jews and deliberately engineered the results Caldwalladr unveiled. It would likewise be silly, however, to suggest that there isn't cause for concern.

What if, for example, an algorithmic system, through recursive deep learning, acquired a racist bias that had not been obvious in the original test data from which it learned because of algorithmic coincidence? We can't say that the system is racist, perhaps, but what does it matter if it behaves in a similar way?

The risk is that algorithmic systems, almost by definition, will ultimately be applied to questions that are similar, but not identical, to the questions they were built to answer. If they weren't, you wouldn't need an algorithmic system. You could just calculate the answer.

Still not convinced of the risk? Consider that Google alone is processing, on average, forty thousand search queries *per second*. That's 3.5 billion searches per day. And, according to Google, 15 percent of those queries, or more than five hundred million per day, are brand-new and have never been asked before. It is statistically certain that at some point someone is going to encounter the same kind of negative bias that Caldwalladr did. And what if that someone is your twelve-year-old son or daughter researching a school project?

The risk of both algorithmic bias and the inability of tech companies like Facebook and Google to control the veracity of the news they disseminate all came to light, of course, during the 2016 US presidential election, when the term "fake news" earned a spot in both the presidential vocabulary and the American lexicon. Politicians are now scrambling to understand and respond.

Any attempt to regulate content, however, is doomed to failure. For starters, you can't remove the bias from algorithms any more than you can eliminate the bias of any human reporter or broadcast company executive. If scientific truths are little more than probabilities shaped by an infinitely variable context, how can we ever expect algorithms to sort it all out? At best they can be designed to catch the blatant lies, and those aren't where the real risks exist. The real risk is that two people are going to look at the same red vegetable, and one is going to call it a to-mah-toe and the other is going to call it a to-may-toe.

Print and broadcast media companies, of course, face the same challenge. And, of course, freedom of the press is protected by the First Amendment to the US Constitution. Regulating media content, as a practical matter, is a nonstarter in a liberal democracy.

None of which was a very big problem when there were several media outlets in virtually every urban area of the country, and it was costly and impractical to ship newspapers over long distances. The media was naturally localized in the same way the population was.

With the advent of radio and television, however, that all changed, and the Federal Communication Commission was created by the Communications Act of 1934 to ensure the integrity of the country's information infrastructure. Given the restrictions of the First Amendment, however, and the natural impediments to arbitrating objectivity, the FCC recognized that the most it could do to ensure media integrity was to ensure competition and prevent monopolies, much as the SEC does in other areas of commerce and business.

Technology, however, favors consolidation because of the high cost to develop and maintain it. While capitalism always favors consolidation over time due to the fulcrums and levers I've talked about, the process is both accelerated and aggravated when the capital costs of entry and expansion are very high. It's almost impossible to promote competition in industries like electric utilities, for example, where the government relies on direct regulation to protect the American consumer.

There is, however, an inherent problem in any attempt at government regulation that is really driven by those same levers and fulcrums we've been talking about, in this case greatly aggravated by the incentive of financial self-interest. All too often, as a result, the regulatory process itself falls into the control of the very companies it is supposed to be regulating. They, of course, are the ones with the expertise the regulatory body needs to perform its duties and, by definition, they ultimately control the flow of data that feeds regulatory knowledge.

When Congress became concerned about the impact online media had on the 2016 presidential election, whom did they call to testify? The executives of Google and Facebook, of course, each of whom have a different incentive than the family in Topeka, Kansas, who just wants to have access to news that is as honest and objective as it can be. (In reality, that's probably not what they want, human psychology being what it is, but that reality doesn't change the issue under discussion so much as it reinforces the need.)

As of April 2017, Google alone processed over 77 percent of all worldwide search queries. And while it is more difficult to measure market share in the social media space given its amorphous definition, the Facebook community is larger than any other on earth. Both far surpass any level of concentration that Adam Smith would have found tolerable in a free capitalist market.

It's time, in other words, to do exactly what Lee Sedol did in game four of his match with AlphaGo. It's time to think outside of the pattern. A pattern exists within a context. If we can't change the pattern itself, we can change the context.

The Internet today is ultimately built in the context of the social, political, and economic models that emphasize the supremacy of the individual. All the arguments currently underway about net neutrality, the deep web, and government firewalls are all defined by the fundamental assumption that the rights of the individual are more important than the rights of the collective. Or, as Thomas Jefferson put it, the former drives the latter. Without freedom of the press, democracy cannot exist.

That was indeed true in Jefferson's day. The press was all there was. The press was the single vehicle by which we all learned about the world around us. (Word of mouth, of course, has always played a role, but it is, by definition, an ineffective method for mass communication.)

That vehicle, moreover, turned on institutions. Jefferson and his fellow Americans at the time got their news from companies like the *Boston Gazette*, the *Pennsylvania Evening Post*, and the *New York Journal*. And while all of these institutions were undoubtedly biased, they adhered to certain standards of journalism designed to protect their public support.

Today, however, we get our news and our opinions from individuals, not institutions. Katy Perry, Justin Bieber, and Taylor Swift, in that order, had the most Twitter followers in 2016. Barack Obama ranked fourth, with only eighty million followers. Trump, as of June, had thirty-two million followers, but Perry became the first person to achieve more than one hundred million followers in the same month.

This personal association, of course, is reinforced by the same technology that relies on the algorithm and its inherent bias. It's all a matter of fame and popularity.

The original promise of digital technology for most social and political observers was the democratization of opinion and influence. The Internet and the social media that helps to drive it give every citizen a microphone. While our personal message was once confined to the crowd we could gather on a street corner or in our living rooms, each of us now has a potentially global audience. In mere seconds our influence can be felt around the world.

Potentially—which, of course, is just another form of probability. Having the ability to be heard, as we now know, is not the same as actually being heard. In 2013 there were already 152 million blogs on the Internet. Web portal statista.com predicts that there will be close to thirty-two million American bloggers alone by 2020.

And how does it all get sorted out? By the numbers, of course. To have your voice heard on the Internet, we all now know, you must win at the game of numbers. Everything turns on fame. And that includes fame for fame itself. In essence, our algorithms create closed-loop feedback systems that, over time, get, by definition, more and more closed. (Open a Twitter account today and see how long it takes you to achieve Katy Perry's one hundred million followers.)

There are many implications. The most obvious, but seldom acknowledged, is that the Internet will eventually implode, along with the companies that drive its traffic. Once Katy Perry has one billion followers, there will be no need to follow anyone else. Once the ten most popular bloggers take over the blogosphere, everyone else will give up.

It won't, of course, be a very pretty picture. Technology won't collapse, but Wall Street will. And the silver lining is that once we put down our smartphones and tablets, we will realize that there is actually another human being sitting next to us. We might even strike up a conversation. And there are all kinds of psychological and sociological reasons why that will be a very good thing indeed.

But this is a book about collectivism. And collectivism is relevant here because it is the only possible way for us to achieve a controlled implosion. We can't stop the digital implosion because technology is just too powerful and the Luddites are not going to win. Nor do we want them to. We can, however, redirect our digital technology in a direction that will not only ease the pain and suffering, but which will liberate technology's ultimate promise.

All we have to do is to start putting the collective good above individual freedom. All we have to do is start putting the "We" above the "I."

And how would that work? To me it is very simple. We have to decommercialize the Internet. We have to start treating it less like the ultimate commercial Ponzi scheme and more like the social resource that it is.

By definition, that means censorship. Yes, it's an ugly word. But it's not an ugly concept when it is applied for the common good. Forget about what people said about the freedom of the press two hundred years ago. That press no longer exists. Our informational reality has changed. Do we really want to give child pornographers, religious radicals, identity thieves, and sexist and racist politicians the same rights we give the fourth-grade teacher educating our children? Do we really want to empower the haters and the cheaters and the bullies among us?

In the famed but rumored words of Deep Throat, if we want the real answer to our problems, we need to "follow the money." And in this case, that means digital advertising. We don't have to ban it, but we do have to regulate it. If we want to repurpose the Internet, we have to change the way we fund it.

Advertisers and the technology platforms that sell them the advertising have done exactly what we incentivized them to do. For the platforms, we have incentivized them to make their platforms as addictive as possible, even if it means exploiting fundamental human vulnerabilities. And for the advertisers, we have allowed them to push the concept of personhood, and the freedom of speech that goes with it in a democracy, further and further down the path that George Orwell, Thomas Jefferson, and thousands, if not millions, of other have warned us about.

Advertisers chase clicks. And that, in turn, tightens the noose of closed-loop reinforcement tighter and tighter. Fame begets fame. The rich get richer. The masses get left behind. It all works on the same principles that any addiction does. We crave for more but can never quite get enough. A circle of death and disaster.

In the end you can still have personal enterprise and creative identity within a collectivist socio-economic-political system. It's all about funding and control. It always is.

The truth is that we have a collectivist system now. If the advertisers fund the Internet, who funds the advertisers? We do, of course. All I'm suggesting is that if we're going to pay for it, we should have some say in how it's managed and for what purpose it exists. We should run things for the social "We," not the corporate "we."

Summary
We must realign our management and application of technology to serve the collective "We."

- We shouldn't be afraid to censor the Internet. Information is always censored anyway. We might as well control the process in the interest of the greater society.
- We need to regulate the Internet in the same way we regulate all media, both in terms of the information it disseminates and the power it gains through concentration. Monopolies, as Adam Smith warned us, are no better in the media than they are in steel.
- We must find a new way to fund the Internet. Advertising will always sacrifice the collective good for the individual financial gain. We are incentivizing companies to addict us.

CHAPTER 9

Education

• • •

*The direction in which education starts a
man will determine his future in life.*

—Plato (427–347 BCE)

*Education is a weapon whose effects depend on who
holds it in his hands and at whom it is aimed.*

—Joseph Stalin (1878–1953)

Perhaps no other variable is more critical to the effective functioning of our interconnected social, political, and economic systems than education. It is essential to social tolerance, a functional democracy, and an advancing modern economy. Never before, in other words, has education been more critical to both our way of life and our standing in the world.

We've all heard about the young titans of Silicon Valley who dropped out of college and went on to become billionaires. They, however, are the exceptions, and, in fact, they were all pretty well educated relative to the average American by the time they got to college.

On the surface, the United States seems to have done pretty well in terms of educating its citizens. According to the US Census Bureau, almost nine out of ten American adults (88 percent) has a high school diploma and a little over half have at least some college education, while approximately one third have a bachelor's degree or higher.

According to leading data provider, Times Higher Education, moreover, seventeen of the top twenty-five and three of the top five universities in the world (2016–2017) are American institutions. All told, according to the Institute of Education Sciences, a branch of the US Department of Education, about twenty million students are attending American colleges and universities as of fall 2017.

Still, given the demands of our political and economic institutions, the one out of ten Americans without a high school diploma or GED, and even the five out of ten Americans without a bachelor's degree, are statistically unlikely to lead comfortable, fulfilling lives. They are at the highest risk for falling into poverty and patterns of self-destructive behavior.

One of the biggest and most fundamental changes impacting our American way of life has been, as previously noted, our loss of access to nature. For much of our existence, nature provided the ultimate safety net for Americans down on their luck or lacking the skills that an education might offer. Virtually all land in the United States is now restricted by ownership and government regulation.

At the same time, advances in agriculture at every level, from mechanization to soil management, have driven agricultural productivity ever higher. While plenty of poor Americans still don't have enough to eat, and nutrition is a national health crisis, the United

States produces more food each year than it can consume, and it does it with fewer people than ever before.

According to the Bureau of Labor Statistics, only 1.5 percent of all American workers are employed in the agriculture, forestry, and fishing industries, and only .5 percent of all American workers are self-employed farmers. At the time of the American Revolution, by contrast, almost 90 percent of Americans were working in agriculture. By 1900, farming employed roughly 40 percent. But as late as 1950, following World War II, more than one in ten Americans was still employed on America's farms.

That's not to suggest for a minute that farming doesn't require knowledge and skill. It surely does. It has historically been, however, the kind of knowledge and skill that was passed down from one generation to another and didn't require an advanced degree. It does today, of course, so that even the relatively few jobs still available in the agriculture sector are largely out of the reach of those lacking a secondary or collegiate education.

But if secondary and collegiate education is increasingly necessary to participate in any but the bottom rungs of the American economy, that education comes at an increasingly higher cost. According to government statistics, the average tuition, fees, room, and board at America's public universities and colleges is now close to $17,000 per year. At a private nonprofit institution of higher learning, the average annual cost exceeds $43,000.

According to a 2017 GOBankingRates survey, however, 39 percent of Americans have no savings at all, and more than half (57 percent) have less than $1,000 in total savings. Only one in four has more than $10,000 socked away.

It's no surprise, therefore, that most students today have to borrow money in order to get the education they need to get ahead at even a modest level. As of 2017, more than forty-four million Americans now hold student loan debt totaling $1.45 trillion.

To put that into perspective, that's almost twice the total US credit card debt. The class of 2016, on average, graduated with $37,172 in student loan debt.

What are we thinking? Forget about fairness; what would Adam Smith say? What impact does this debt have on overall American productivity, mental health, and the health of our social institutions? To say nothing about the American savings rate, which, in theory, is the source of the capital America needs to move the economy forward. How can we expect young Americans to work hard, save, and volunteer in the community when they are literally drowning in student loan debt?

And for those free-market capitalists who argue that those students agreed to take on that debt, I say we should legalize heroin. Of course they agreed to it. What choice did they have? And, by the way, these are young adults who have virtually no experience in managing personal finances or structuring a personal balance sheet. It's inhumane, and it's bad business.

The student debt market, incidentally, is not subject to Smith's invisible hand of market efficiency. The vast majority of that student debt is guaranteed by the American taxpayer. Which is why American banks have behaved so irrationally in doling it out. It's a sure win for them. They could not care less that loan delinquency rates now exceed 11 percent. They're still getting their fees.

Which is also to say that the American taxpayer is helping to foot the outsized salaries, bonuses, and benefits now enjoyed by America's bankers who are, of course, too big to fail once their poor decisions reach crisis levels.

The bottom line, to put it in banker lingo, is that a college education should be free of charge for every American that can earn his or her way in. Without free education, we are going to drag our economy, our social institutions, and our democracy into a deeper and deeper abyss. The polarization of wealth will continue to accelerate, social injustice will continue to be the norm, and we will bear witness to the first generation in American history to lead less secure and comfortable lives than their parents.

And disregard every politician who claims we can't afford it. We're going to pay for it one way or the other. The American taxpayer is paying for it now, and the load is going to get worse, much worse, until we change the trajectory.

But access to education, of course, is only part of the overall educational challenge we face in the twenty-first century. An equal, if not bigger challenge, is the quality of the education we do provide.

We must first, of course, make a quality education equally accessible to everyone. The No Child Left Behind Act took a step in that direction by requiring all schools meet standardized testing.

It is, however, the way we fund our schools that is really at the heart of the problem. In funding our schools largely through local real estate taxes, we have created another self-reinforcing closed-loop system that ultimately divides and polarizes the educational offering. Housing costs in the good school systems rises, the local schools get more funding, there is more competition to live there, housing costs continue to rise, and the polarizing loop is in place. While one community is on its way up, another is on its way down.

That doesn't mean that every school district should be rewarded with the same budget or that parents shouldn't have some freedom to send their children to the best schools. What we have now, however, isn't working.

While measuring education effectiveness is difficult, according to Pearson rankings issued in 2014, the world's top five education systems belong to South Korea, Japan, Singapore, Hong Kong, and Finland. The United Kingdom and Canada ranked sixth and seventh, respectively, and the United States ranked fourteenth, just behind Russia and Germany. According to a more recent report issued by the World Economic Forum in 2016, the United States ranked as the eighth most educated country in the world, behind Norway, Denmark, Belgium, Switzerland, Netherlands, Finland, and Singapore.

This isn't explained by aggregate funding. The United States spends more on education than any other country on the planet. And the unions are not to blame. We need more unions like the teachers' unions, not fewer. Teaching remains one of the most underpaid professions in the United States today.

What we do need to stop, however, is the absurd practice of state licensing of the professions, including teaching. The state licensing bureaus, which regulate everything from who can cut hair and give manicures to who can teach our children, are a huge source of income for the states, and the work they do, always in the name of consumer protection, serves only to create oligopolies and perpetuate poverty.

Do barbers really need to have five thousand hours of training at an accredited for-profit barber school before we can trust the invisible hand of market forces to weed out the good barbers from the bad ones, as is the case in California and many other states? Where does this need to protect consumers from bad haircuts come from? Look around—it's not working, and it's draining resources from the system, dampening overall economic activity, and denying the impoverished another possible route out of their poverty.

The case for certifying teachers, of course, is stronger. They are, after all, teaching the very people that our society, our economy, and our political institutions will rely on in the future. We need to set the standard high.

But we need to set a high standard of performance, not the right to teach. In most states today, teachers cannot be licensed to teach without passing standardized exams and satisfying the educational requirements of the state, including the completion of course work by a state-approved educational provider. And while the purpose of such mandates is the quality of the education provided, no one benefits quite so much as the state-approved educators, many of which are for-profit institutions ultimately trying to make a buck.

The downside of such a restrictive system is that it greatly and artificially constricts the pool of potential teachers. To get a certificate, you pretty much have to commit to the profession at a young age, and it probably doesn't make sense for anyone not planning to make teaching a lifetime career.

I can think of no other career that would be more attractive to more potential candidates than teaching. New college graduates looking to spend a few years teaching before they move into careers in business or the law. Business executives looking to transition into retirement. People looking to make a difference in the community without committing their careers to teaching. Retired professional athletes.

Wouldn't you like to have Bill Gates or Elon Musk teach your child's tenth grade science class? It's not going to happen, even if they were willing to do it for a few years.

The people already in the closed loop, of course, will argue that we would be filling our teacher ranks with incompetents, pedophiles, and drug dealers. That, of course, is doubtful, but can be guarded against by far less onerous certification requirements. We might, for example, have accredited team leaders who are responsible for ensuring that the teachers in their care have those basic skills that are truly unique to teaching. Standardized testing is also fine, so long as it's not simply a convention to allow a group of people or institutions to pursue an agenda of self-interest—like making money—that has no offsetting collective benefit.

At the very least, the certification process should not be left to the states. That greatly enhances the cost of managing the teaching profession and inhibits professional mobility. To certify teachers in only one state is absurd given current demands for geographic mobility. And it certainly ties Smith's invisible hand that is, in theory, at the heart of American free-market efficiency.

But there is another facet of the certification and curriculum debate that is even more important than the negative impact of state-sponsored oligopolies. What to teach?

There has always been a raging debate among educators, parents, and future employers about what to teach in our primary and secondary schools. Should we teach the three R's? Should we give the children unlikely to go to college more technical skills to prepare them for the modern job market? Or should we simply help children to find their own abilities and educational needs?

The obvious answer is that we need all and none of the above. When it comes to education, we must become, first and foremost, lifelong students. The skill to learn, and to learn productively and with an open mind, is the most important skill we can give our children today.

It is impossible to predict how young people will make a living in the future. The only thing we can say with certainty is that it will require knowledge, it will require collaborating with others, and their jobs will be obsolete before they are ready to retire.

Do you want your daughter to become a skilled coder so that she can develop new apps for the next generation of smartphones? Guess what? Smartphones won't exist in the not-too-distant future. And all of the programming will be performed by artificially intelligent systems.

Perhaps a career in medicine or the law? What is the one common denominator to both professions? They deal in patterns. Doctors diagnose disease based on an informed process of elimination. Lawyers prepare briefs based on their knowledge of precedent. And patterns, of course, are what computers excel at.

And that's just one source of change. If you wanted to be a doctor two or three decades ago, becoming a cardiologist was probably a pretty sound choice. We all have hearts, right? We can't live without them. We can, however, maintain them more efficiently and more effectively through advancements in pharmacology. And the machines can read the electrocardiograms. Patterns, remember.

Nephrologists will continue to be in big demand for the foreseeable future because of the rising epidemic of diabetes. Eventually, however, the pharmacologists will figure it out, and robots will be able to do the dialysis.

The need for the skilled trades will probably last longer that the need for doctors or lawyers only because the machines can learn, but they can't build themselves yet. That day is coming, but probably not for a while.

In the meantime, what can we say with any certainty about the future of employment in the United States? The one thing we can say for certain is that we will live longer. And our political, economic, and social systems will become increasingly integrated, blurring the lines between them. And someone will have to keep an eye on the machines to make sure they don't do something unexpected, just as AlphaGo did in game two of its match with Lee Sedol; only this time, perhaps, the machine decides to terminate its opponent as the surest path to victory.

Many parents and educators have looked at this future and decided that what students need is more training in the STEM subjects—science, technology, engineering, and math. And that's probably not a bad idea. It does, however, only address one side of the need.

What we need more than anything else from people entering the workforce and adulthood are ethics, the skill to collaborate and work with others, social tolerance, the ability to think strategically and at multiple levels and on multiple fronts concurrently, and, above all else, the ability to learn effectively and efficiently.

Here's what the experts have to say. (Taken from a May 3, 2017 article, "How to Prepare for an Automated Future," in the *New York Times* by Claire Cain Miller.)

- At universities, "people learn how to approach new things, ask questions and find answers, deal with new situations," wrote Uta Russmann, a professor of communications at the FHWien University of Applied Sciences in Vienna. "All this is needed to adjust to ongoing changes in work life. Special skills for a particular job will be learned on the job."
- "Many of the 'skills' that will be needed are more like personality characteristics, like curiosity, or social skills that require enculturation to take hold," wrote Stowe Boyd, managing director of Another Voice, which provides research on the new economy.

Are we prepared? Clearly not. Our educational paradigm, like our political and economic paradigms, is stuck in a world that no longer exists.

Summary

We must make a quality education accessible to all, and we must realign the education agenda with the future needs of our collective systems.

- We must find new ways to fund education in both sourcing and allocation.
- A college education should be free to all who qualify.
- We should manage education at the national level to promote consistency, efficiency, and mobility.
- We should develop and promote an educational agenda that emphasizes ethics, compassion, collaboration, and the ability to learn for a lifetime.

CHAPTER 10

Private Property

• • •

As soon the land of any country has all become private property, the landlords, like all other men, love to reap where they never sowed, and demand a rent even for its natural produce.

—Adam Smith (1723–1790)

Our private property must be sacrificed.

—Dolley Madison (1768–1849)
Former First Lady of the United States

There is no single principle more fundamental to the American way of life and American identity that the right to own private property.

Six individuals or their families each own more than one million acres of land in the United States today. John Malone, the chairman of Liberty Media Corp., owns 2.2 million acres, an area two and a half times the state of Rhode Island.

According to a February 15, 2016, article posted on inequality.org, the top five private American landowners, all white men, collectively own more rural land than the entire African American population combined.

Of course the federal government is already the largest landowner in the United States, holding title to some 640 million acres. That's about 28 percent of the country's total surface area, but is heavily skewed toward the western states. The federal government owns 85 percent of the land in Nevada, 53 percent of the land in Oregon, and 50 percent of the land in Idaho, but only 0.4 percent of the land in Connecticut and Rhode Island and less than 2 percent of the land in Massachusetts and Ohio.

Most Americans assume that property rights arrived on our shores with the arrival of European immigrants. That's not entirely accurate, however. Many historians now believe that the Native American tribes living in what would eventually become the United States did abide by an informal system of property rights, particularly relating to the best hunting grounds. And the Europeans' systems of property, of course, were largely built around the feudal system in which the various monarchs of Europe held title to all of the land. The vassals who worked the land did so with much the same practical rights as subsequent American sharecroppers during the Reconstruction era.

John Locke (1632–1704) was an influential English philosopher and physician who wrote the *Two Treatises of Government* in 1690. They ultimately gave rise to the modern notion of liberalism that governs most Western democracies, including the United States, to this day.

Locke and others argued that land and the resources it held existed in a natural state preexisting humankind and, in fact, the original settlers in Plymouth and Jamestown initially chose collective land ownership as the model for their communities. The Puritans, of course, who greatly influenced the future course of the United

States, believed that land and its bounty was a gift from God, and while humanity had dominion over it, the ownership issue was more or less irrelevant.

It is important to note, moreover, that Locke supported the individual appropriation of common property through the application of individual labor. This is a more benign version of appropriation by conquest or discovery, which, of course, had been around since humanity emerged from the savannahs of Africa. The right to trade land as one would trade a trinket purchased in the local market, however, didn't come until much later.

In its 1823 ruling in *Johnson v. M'Intosh*, one of the seminal cases in American land law still studied in law schools today, the US Supreme Court ruled that private citizens did not have the right to purchase lands directly from Native Americans, essentially reserving the right to such transfers for the state. And over time, of course, the courts gradually consolidated and expanded personal property rights to create the system we have today.

This is typical of a liberal democracy. In order to protect the rights of the individual, which are supreme in a democracy, the courts are granted significant power to interpret law. And inevitably that frontier of power becomes blurred beyond recognition: the power to interpret law ultimately becomes the de facto power to make law.

That democratic jurisprudence inevitably assumes more and more power is a function of the courts' emphasis on language. As noted many times, language is an arbitrary human convention that is imprecise and living—it changes in response to the social, economic, and political developments of the day. While we say that the courts are truly independent, they are, in reality, no more independent than our political institutions. Which means, of course, that they are greatly influenced by concentrations of wealth.

This is key. In the end it doesn't really matter who owns the land. Whether it's owned collectively by the people or by individual private citizens changes little. However it came to be, the land exists as part of the natural world. We can destroy the environment it supports, and we can even redistribute it. We can't, however, create it.

What we can control, and what really matters, is what we do with it. And in the United States, the way we manage and control land use reflects the way we manage and control everything else. The individual reigns supreme.

That worked pretty well in the early days of the republic. We had plenty of land, relatively few people, and we had not yet developed the technology that would allow us to consume or destroy it. Land was a great way to motivate people to do things like settle the West. And it reflected the fundamental belief in the dignity of all men, not just the men who wore the crowns or the robes.

There have always been limits, however, and those limits, in one way, have expanded over time through the government's power of eminent domain, zoning laws, regulatory requirements concerning, for example, the environment, and the stronger policing of criminal activity.

Here's what the US Department of Justice has to say about eminent domain:

> The federal government's power of eminent domain has long been used in the United States to acquire property for public use. Eminent domain "appertains to every independent government. It requires no constitutional recognition; it is an attribute of sovereignty." *Boom Co. v. Patterson*, 98 US 403, 406 (1879). However, the Fifth Amendment to the United States Constitution stipulates: "nor shall private property be taken for public use, without just

compensation." Thus, whenever the United States acquires a property through eminent domain, it has a constitutional responsibility to justly compensate the property owner for the fair market value of the property. See *Bauman v. Ross*, 167 US 548 (1897); *Kirby Forest Industries, Inc. v. United States*, 467 US 1, 9–10 (1984). (https://www.justice.gov/enrd/history-federal-use-eminent-domain)

Zoning laws, by contrast, came into being much later. The earliest zoning laws in the United States originated in Los Angeles in 1908. New York City adopted its first zoning regulations in 1916. And, of course, zoning laws have been before the courts ever since.

Further restrictions on land use expanded into the private sector through the homeowner association (HOA). While first developed in the nineteenth century, they came into widespread use in the 1960s when America moved to the suburbs. According to the Community Associations Institute, in 2010 HOAs governed almost twenty-five million American homes and more than sixty million residents.

Over time, however, a land management paradox has emerged. Both the individual and the government have essentially acquired more power. And the result, not surprisingly, is a standoff, or, depending on your perspective, paralysis.

Public and private individuals and entities now compete, largely in the courts, to control land use. And the net result, more often than not, is that money wins. Land has been essentially removed from the collective balance sheet and now exists largely for the benefit of the powerful elite. And that elite, of course, is not defined by merit, intellect, or integrity. It's defined by power and that means, of course, money.

However we do it, and I'm happy to leave the methodology to others, we must take land use management out of the hands of the powerful elite. We must recognize the basic principle that land belongs ultimately to the natural world and should be managed for the collective good.

We have to stop believing that discrete plots of land, however small or large, exist in an environmental or social vacuum. They don't. The world is too crowded, integrated, and mutually dependent to think of land as private property in the same way we think of personal effects and the tradable products of our individual labor.

If a private bank today acquires a property through foreclosure, it essentially has the right to liquidate that property at any price. And for a big bank with billions of dollars in assets, it's an immaterial decision. If it only gets pennies on the dollars, the CEO's bonus is unlikely to be impacted.

But what about the neighbors? Anyone who has ever owned property knows that property values are determined collectively. When the house next door is sold for pennies on the dollar, you will be impacted. And the impact on you will be much greater than the impact on the big bank that is too big to fail.

Perhaps most importantly, we must introduce the element of time. The rights of land usage, however defined, must be contingent upon original intent. If an individual, corporate, or government entity is granted the right to use land in a certain way, the right should not be eternal, and the entity issuing the right should have the authority to rescind it should the original intent not materialize.

The overriding conceptual change in perspective between what we have now and the collectivist state that I envision is the recognition that the world we live in today is a fluid one. It doesn't stand still, and the rights we acquire or are granted shouldn't either. In managing our world and our environment, we are managing a conceptually living entity.

The same must be said, in fact, of all property rights. In addition to land-use rights, intellectual property rights must exist and be managed within the same fundamental perspective and framework.

Who owns an idea? The person who comes up with it? How do we know who that is? How does he or she know? And how does anyone know that the idea isn't obvious and that others weren't on the verge of discovering it?

I am a writer. I am, more specifically, a writer who is sixty-three years old. And I am a writer who has flown well in excess of a million miles, reads roughly one hundred books per year, and has sat through more corporate meetings than I care to recall. I have a bachelor's degree in economics, and I have attended countless seminars and training sessions.

Where do my ideas come from? I have no idea. I am obviously a product of my own unique experience and that experience feels highly personal. But it's not, and it never has been. I am the product of every person I have ever met—every teacher, every boss, every colleague, everyone. It is absurd to suggest that I even know where I leave off and my context begins. They are one and the same.

This past week, as I write this, the federal government passed a $1.3 trillion tax reform package. And, of course, the news dominated the news cycle, both for and against.

The pro side of the media, of course, argued that corporate tax cuts were good for Americans because they would trigger growth in jobs and wages. And one of the arguments frequently given in support of that scenario was the fact that US companies are often competing against foreign companies that are subsidized by their jurisdictional government. One commentator noted, for example, that Boeing, one of the companies that saw fit to express their glee publicly, competed against Airbus, and that the latter benefited from government subsidies while the former did not.

Are you kidding me? How stupid do these commentators think we are? Where would Boeing be if no city or municipality saw fit to build or maintain an airport? Where would the company be if the US government stopped funding education? Health care? The country's defense? The police? The highways they use to transport parts?

No entity exists in a vacuum. And that reality has never been more true than it is today. Ideas are the currency of our society, our economy, and our democracy. Who can honestly say where they come from and who, for whatever reason, should enjoy ownership rights to them?

The issue has never been more important or more relevant. Consider this quote from an article in the *New York Times* in 2012:

> In the smartphone industry alone, according to a Stanford University analysis, as much as $20 billion was spent on patent litigation and patent purchases in the last two years—an amount equal to eight Mars rover missions. Last year, for the first time, spending by Apple and Google on patent lawsuits and unusually big-dollar patent purchases exceeded spending on research and development of new products, according to public filings.

> "The Patent, Used as a Sword"
> *New York Times*
> Charles Duhigg and Steve Lohr
> October 7, 2012

And who paid for that $20 billion in non-value-added litigation? You did, of course. You are paying for the Silicon Valley ecosystem that exploits collective idea generation in the interest of creating another tech billionaire. It's starting to sound a bit feudal, don't you think?

Patent and other intellectual property rights are not natural and were not granted by God, if you believe in one. They were developed as far back as medieval times in recognition of the fact that some ideas required substantial sums of money to develop and apply, and people and companies would not make rational decisions to do that if they had no reasonable expectation that they could recoup the investment.

That's fine. That, in the limited sense originally intended, continues to make sense. What doesn't make sense, however, is to allow intellectual property laws to be exploited by individuals and corporations as a competitive weapon. Nor should we allow intellectual property to morph from a practical accommodation into a prized financial asset.

As in the case of land-use rights, intellectual property rights should exist and be managed in the interests of the collective good. That's ultimately where they came from anyway.

Summary

We must rethink personal property. How it's owned is largely irrelevant. What matters is how it's used and how we manage that use to ensure collective benefit.

* However land-use rights are administered, they should be administered in the interests of the collective good.

- Land-use rights should exist in the context of time. The right should not be eternal, and the failure to execute original intent should potentially eliminate the right acquired.
- Patent and other intellectual property rights should be of limited duration and should not be tradable without regulatory approval that is wielded in the public interest.
- Corporations that exist for the simple purpose of holding patents and other intellectual property should be prohibited.

PART III
Political
∙ ∙ ∙

CHAPTER 11

Rule of Law

• • •

No organic law can ever be framed with provisions specifically applicable to every question which may occur in practical administration. No foresight can anticipate nor any document of reasonable length contain express provisions for all possible questions.

—Abraham Lincoln (1809–1865)
First Inaugural Address
March 4, 1861

As you must know by now, I believe that one of the most significant and unappreciated aspects of our modern reality is the arbitrary and imprecise nature of language. It is a human convention designed to promote the effectiveness and efficiency of communication. At best, however, the results are mixed.

It is often said that we live in a postindustrial information age and that is indeed true. We often fail to recognize the significance of that reality, however.

When we use language to control the behavior of others, either through written laws and regulations or spoken demands, we create a duality. Simply put, in saying something we are not saying something else. And the implications are enormous.

This is particularly true in a liberal democratic capitalist state, where words carry more weight than they do under any form of governance designed to organize our culture, our economy, and our politics. We call it the rule of law, but it is, at its heart, the rule of words.

The legislative branch of government, of course, is given the authority to write those laws. The administrative branch is charged with administering them. And the judicial branch—the courts—interprets them. It all sounds very rational and virtuous. But it is only rational to the extent that words are expressively precise and all-encompassing. And the reality is that as our world gets smaller, more crowded, and more technologically advanced, the precision and relative breadth of words and their meaning erodes constantly.

Many Americans, for example, used to believe that God created the world in seven days. Some still do. But many no longer accept the creationist story. As science and culture have evolved, alternative beliefs have come to be more and more widely accepted.

That is true, in fact, of all dogma. The laws of entropy apply as much to the world of thought as they do to the natural world. New ideas emerge; old ideas are challenged and lose sway.

The Greek philosopher Pyrrho of Elis, who lived in the fourth century BCE and traveled to India with the armies of Alexander the Great, truly understood the limitations of language and dogma. He believed that all dogma was ultimately flawed and recommended that it all be ignored. Ultimately, this conclusion gave birth to the philosophical school of skepticism.

Dogma, as the word is used today, is any tenet that is not authoritatively true. While many people today mistakenly interpret that to mean any and all knowledge that is not confirmed by the scientific method, virtually all judgments are dogmatic, even if the scientific method was the path you followed to get there.

Pyrrho intuitively (The scientific method had not been articulated yet.) understood this reality and rejected all judgment. He was, you might say, skeptical of skepticism itself. He called this expanded skepticism *ataraxia*. Which, anecdotally, made for an interesting life. His aides, legend has it, had to stay with him at all times because even the judgment that walking off a cliff would lead to bodily harm would have been rejected by Pyrrho.

In the world of philosophy, the suspension of all judgment is now called *epoché*. It flows from the paradox that what we know and how we know it cannot be known independently, thus precluding a definitive answer to either question. In the field of epistemology, it is known as the problem of the criterion.

So now fast-forward to a country of 315 million people governed by the rule of law, and you begin to understand the problem. Rules are not meant to be broken, as they say, as much as they are meant to be interpreted in the most desirable way.

That's where the lawyers come in. Their job is to press the interpretation of whoever is paying them. And Pyrrho would have hated them even more than Shakespeare apparently did.

A law or regulation is meant to influence behavior through the written word. The moment a law is passed, however, the second-guessing begins. What does this word really mean? What was the real intent of this clause? It says this, but doesn't say that, so that must be OK.

In a court of law, we call them technicalities. Where regulations are involved, we call them loopholes. Where someone wants to do something that the government wanted to prevent, they call it the gift of language.

All of which, of course, costs money to sort out. And, by definition, the people who need the most money are the elected officials, who need money to win elections. And they get it, more often than not, from the wealthy individuals and corporations who have the money in the first place. Either way, the rich folks win. And they win virtually every time.

Under the American system, one of three things happens:

- In an effort to close loopholes and diminish the use of technicalities to avert intent, the legislators add more words. Eventually, however, the laws and regulations become so complicated that they are impractical for the politicians themselves to write. They're politicians, not technocrats. And they have to spend their time preparing for reelection. As a result, they turn over the actually writing of the laws and regulations to the very people who they are meant to be writing them to protect against. They have both the time (because they have the interest) and they have the "expertise." At this point, they can write the technicalities and loopholes directly into the legislation, eliminating the time and cost of having to go to the courts.
- The laws and regulations become so complex that no one understands them and they aren't, as a practical matter, enforced. The intent isn't realized, and the commitment to the rule of law is undermined. Eventually, all laws and regulations are essentially ignored.
- A situation arises that all parties agree was not foreseen when the law or regulation was passed. As Lincoln noted, this is inevitable, and due to the growing complexity of our social, economic, and political institutions, it happens more and more with each passing day. In this case we either force the politicians or the wealthy elite to rewrite or challenge the law, or, in the vernacular of the day, we screw the little guy in a way that everyone agrees doesn't make sense. "Sorry, it's the law. I didn't write it. I just enforce it."

Even back in the 1700s, when everything was a lot less integrated and complex, and there were only a relative handful of us to govern, the Founding Fathers recognized this potential perversion of the system. So they created a stopgap—trial by a jury of peers.

The trial by a jury of peers doctrine is the foundation of the American legal system. It is not, however, a democratic institution. Many modern liberal democracies utilize the jury system far less extensively than the United States.

The United States, however, is the sweet spot of individual rights and freedoms so the jury system is conceptually attractive. And in the context of eighteenth-century America, it probably worked quite well, at least in the political and social context of the times.

Jury selection was delegated to the states and every state limited the right to men, and three states restricted the right to white men only. Except Vermont, that is, which restricted jury service to property owners or taxpayers (essentially white men).

The Federal Judiciary Act of 1789 delegated the power to establish juror qualifications to the states, and many states aligned the qualifications for jury service with the qualifications to vote. That meant, of course, that juries were not in any way democratically selected, as we would now define the term.

> Many states, however, imposed additional requirements—both general requirements of intelligence, good character, and the like and specific taxpaying and property-holding requirements.
>
> "History of the Criminal Jury"
> *The University of Chicago Law Review*, 1994
> Albert Alschuler & Andrew G. Deiss

In another example of legal entropy, the courts have, over time, eroded the most discriminatory qualifications for jury service, but the system remains far from representative in terms of any democratic ideal. Under the supervision of public officials known as selectmen or supervisors, jury pools are typically drawn from either voter registration records or the pool of residents who hold a state driver's license.

At the same time, of course, the United States has grown bigger, more populated, and more technologically advanced. There is virtually no way to determine if a group of jurors selected from the voter registration rolls has the self-knowledge that will be relied upon in the determination of fact. In any but the most straightforward case, which we probably don't need a jury to decide anyway, it is doubtful that the jurors will have the experience or expertise to evaluate the facts objectively or accurately.

That, of course, has given rise to the "expert witness" who, in theory, does have the necessary expertise. To the extent that juries rely on the testimony of expert witnesses, however, the democratic nature of the jury trial has already been compromised. And, of course, since expert witnesses are less closely regulated than say, judges, and operate to the rules of the free market in charging for their time and testimony, the door has been opened to outright bribery and misrepresentation and, even if that is not true, power has again shifted in favor of the wealthy elite who can obviously afford the best expert witnesses.

But while it would be good to have jurors who were informed in the subject matter at hand, we don't want jurors who are generally informed, meaning we don't want jurors who are already familiar with a case and probably, as a result, have already reached a tentative conclusion regarding guilt before the case is even heard.

And, again, in the 1700s it probably wasn't all that difficult to find uninformed jurors. Citizens, in general, were less informed simply because people were less informed about the news of the day.

In an era of smartphones, the twenty-four seven news cycle, and social media, however, is it even possible to find a jury that has not been tainted by pretrial publicity? And the degree to which potential jurors are tainted, of course, is greatly exaggerated by the fact that we all get our news from self-reinforcing sources.

In August 2017, the Pew Research Center conducted a survey that found that two-thirds (67 percent) of Americans now report that they get at least some of their news from social media. And in a finding that surprised everyone, more than half of Americans (55 percent) over the age of fifty now admit to getting news from social media. And, Pew found, 69 percent of Americans without a college degree now rely on social media for their news, an increase of nine percentage points in just one year.

In a degree of economic concentration that would surely alarm Adam Smith himself, were he alive, one company—Facebook—dominates social media news. Pew found that 65 percent of all Americans use the site for social media, but that 45 percent, almost half, of all Americans get their news there. If any other news source reached anything like that degree of concentration, the Justice Department would have broken it up yesterday.

Consider the degree to which identity politics now influences all of our social, economic, and political institutions. Identity politics is, by definition, biased politics. It can come at the bias from either direction—for or against—but that doesn't change the reality that bias exists.

This not only compromises the democratic "fairness" of the American legal system, it literally perverts justice. How? Because few criminal defendants, and virtually no civil defendants, wants to put their fate in the hands of a jury of peers.

According to government statistics, more than nine out of ten criminal defendants plead guilty before actually going to trial. In civil cases, only three out of one hundred actually goes before the jury.

Part of the reason, of course, is that a jury trial is very expensive for the state to pursue. The jurors and the state's experts all have to be paid. To say nothing of the courtroom and the people who work there. Or the even larger cost of maintaining the infrastructure of jury justice. Throw in the lost productivity resulting from potential jurors who are taken away from their productive employment, and the cost must easily run in the billions of dollars per year.

But if the state and the defendants both want to avoid a jury trial because the results are so unpredictable, it is an avoidance that greatly empowers the state. Innocent defendants plead guilty to crimes they did not commit every day in America because they know that going to trial poses an even bigger risk.

Prosecutors understand their power well. If a criminal defendant is unwilling to plead guilty at the level they desire, they up the ante and bring additional charges. Or, conversely, district attorneys, who are themselves elected and thus reliant on the support of wealthy citizens, reduce charges for well-connected citizens.

Once again, them that has, gets. The wealthy and powerful elite are able to scam the system in their favor. The poor and the helpless get lost in the system.

It's just another example of democratic exploitation by paradox. A system that is, in theory, designed to empower and protect the individual, in practice protects only some individuals, usually at the expense of the common majority.

SUMMARY

We must put justice back into the American legal system.

- Judges must be removed from the political process in the same way that the Supreme Court and other federal judges are.
- We must rethink the entire system of jury trials.
- The power of independent and unaccountable courts to interpret law to the extent of making law needs to be contained. How is up for debate.
- There should be a principle of common sense, however defined, that all laws and regulations are subordinate to.

CHAPTER 12

Unintended Consequences

• • •

Oops.

—Anonymous

One of the most significant pieces of wisdom that I've picked up over my six-plus decades of roaming the earth is that sometimes the dog just don't hunt.

Human history is a voluminous tale of one group of people trying to influence the behavior of another group of people. They want them to do something or behave in a certain way; or not to do something else and behave in a different way; or buy something; or just plain think and speak the same way they do.

Sometimes it works, of course. And sometimes it works on a scale that you just can't comprehend until after the fact. Often it doesn't, however, and the price can be very steep. But whether it works or not, it never lasts. The world just won't stand still. The universe inevitably falls back on the cosmic sine wave of change.

Newton's third law of physics states that for every action there is an equal and opposite reaction. It's true, but the implications are bigger than the original truth.

If science has taught us anything since Newton's day, it is that the universe is integrated in a way he could never have imagined. Virtually nothing exists or happens in isolation. Everything, in effect, is a vast integrated ecosystem, including the social and economic systems in which political governance takes place. Climate change, racism, the polarization of wealth, war, and misogyny are all interrelated at some level. Even now we don't quite comprehend the full extent of it.

This reality, in turn, gives rise to the law of unintended consequences, the reaction side of Newton's original law. It arises because the initial action that Newton refers to is often not easy to isolate, much less articulate through the imprecise convention of language. When we do X, in other words, we are probably defining only one aspect of X. The rest of X, in the end, creates unintended consequences.

There is a time element as well. The rest of X, and thus much of Y, the reaction, may not be immediately apparent. It takes time, often through perpetual self-reinforcement, to reach the critical mass that calls it to our attention. Eventually those reactions reach a tipping point, and things start to turn back in the other direction, often with a big nudge once we realize the full implications of the original action.

When applied to economics, culture, and politics, as a result, the sinusoidal performance or action/reaction curve defines many aspects of how we live over time. The ongoing economic cycles of expansion and recession are the most obvious and well understood, but Newton's third law applies equally to all aspects of our collective culture and governance. It's at the heart of trends in everything from fashion to scientific research.

It further explains why all attempts at social engineering come with big inherent risks. Whatever action we take will have a profound impact that we seldom fully understand ahead of time. And even to the extent we do, the self-reinforcing behavior of all action over time often unfolds at different rates among the many facets, some unknown, of the original action.

In essence, the second law of thermodynamics, which defines the universality of entropy, meets Newton's third law, creating the law of unintended consequence, which, in turn, defines the universal law of sinusoidal patterns of actions and reactions.

Governance, above all else, is the relentless pursuit of social engineering, or, perhaps more accurately, reengineering. The American political campaign is, in the end, a promise to interfere. Even if a particular political candidate promises to get the government off our backs, he or she can only do that by interfering.

Sometimes this interference is obvious and proactive. Let's look at the government's role in promoting home ownership in the United States as an example.

Following World War II, America's developers built the suburbs that now define, in large part, the American way of life. In 1950 only one in four Americans lived in the suburbs. Today more than half of us do.

Developers, on the surface, built those suburbs. But it was the government that truly empowered the trend. The suburbs wouldn't exist if the government hadn't built the infrastructure necessary to support them, ensured the availability of cheap gasoline, and promoted home and car ownership through tax incentives, plentiful consumer credit, and supportive banking regulations. In the case of housing, the government also created Fannie Mae and Freddie Mac, two government-sponsored enterprises that are now in conservatorship and run by the Federal Housing Finance Agency (FHFA).

While all of this proactive government social engineering has helped to bring the American dream to life, there have been many unintended consequences, many of which we are now paying dearly for. Chief among them, of course, has been the United States' role in the climate change that now threatens our very existence. The suburban home, and the personal automobile it requires, are both inefficient models of energy consumption.

But the unintended consequences don't stop there. The suburban migration empowered racial segregation, income, educational, and health-care inequality, illegal drug use, crime, religious intolerance, and a level of personal isolation that we now know is unhealthy and contributes to social division, depression, substance abuse, a rising suicide rate, and general disillusionment.

The social engineering designed to promote home ownership has been successful, however. Before World War II, less than half of Americans (43.6 percent) owned their own home (US Census Bureau). Today, however, more than two-thirds of the population is living the dream of home ownership. This, of course, occurred at a time when the United States population more than doubled, from 132 million people in 1940, to 315 million people today.

Due to the methods employed, however, and the unintended consequences of racism and income inequality that resulted, the United States ranks only forty-first in the world in terms of home ownership today. The top five, in fact, with the exception of Singapore, are all current or former Communist countries, where home ownership rates exceed 90 percent.

Sometimes, of course, the social engineering results from the government's failure to act. The union membership rate in the United States, for example, has declined by half since 1983, all of it, ironically, in the private sector. The workers didn't destroy the unions; the government did by failing to uphold the spirit of the National Labor Relations Act of 1935 and otherwise supporting, often through inaction, corporate union busters, in the same way it enabled the destruction of corporate pensions and employment-based health insurance.

These are not, moreover, isolated examples of government social engineering gone bad or coming up short. Nancy Reagan told us to "Just Say No." And now, of course, we have a national epidemic in opioid abuse and heroin addiction. Prohibition, in the name of sobriety, gave us bootleggers and helped to strengthen organized crime, just as the war on drugs strengthened the drug cartels and the war on vice does as much to empower the pimps and sex traffickers as it does to promote morality among the nation's youth.

Social engineering, however, is not limited to the government sector. Corporations use it, too, to promote their self-interests.

Richard H. Thaler, professor of Economics and Behavioral Science at the University of Chicago's Graduate School of Business, was awarded the 2017 Nobel Prize in Economics for his work in "understanding the psychology of economics." In 2009 he coauthored a book with Cass R. Sunstein entitled *Nudge: Improving Decisions About Health, Wealth, and Happiness.* In it the authors introduced their concept of "libertarian paternalism," a form of deliberate choice architecture. In essence, the authors advocate for nudging individual choices in ways that promote an ideal goal (paternalism) but are otherwise cheap in cost, modest in sacrifice, and easy to avoid (libertarian).

It's ultimately a book about social engineering. And, as the authors point out, we are constantly being nudged whether we recognize it or not. When you stand in front of a retail display to choose your brand of toothpaste, for example, you are being not-so-subtly nudged by very deliberate decisions on product placement. And it works. You will buy, on average, the exact toothpaste you have been subconsciously programmed to buy.

The retailer and the manufacturers that supply it, in this case, are nudging your decision in ways that you are not even aware of, both through signage at the point-of-sale and where the product is placed on the shelf. As in real estate, location is everything. Place the product on the top or bottom shelf, and it will sit. Place it at eye level with an attention-grabbing shelf sticker, and you've got a potential best seller.

But nudging costs money. And it's ultimately built into the cost of the product, meaning that we—the citizens, consumers, and taxpayers—are picking up the bill for a process that, in the end, has no redeeming value for us as individuals or society at large.

Advertising, while huge (roughly $150 billion per year in the United States), is just the tip of the iceberg. Many retailers charge manufacturers "slotting fees" just to carry their product. And if you want your product displayed at eye level or on an endcap, you're probably going to pay extra. Some manufacturers, particularly in the grocery business, also hire armies of people to go into the stores and secure the best display positions and adorn them with shelf cards, floor stickers, and other devices to nudge the consumer in the direction of a purchase. The money changes hands between the manufacturer and the retailer, but it ultimately comes out of your pocket.

Product marketing, including advertising, is justified under the general heading of market efficiency. If consumers are expected to behave rationally, as Adam Smith assumed in his advocacy of free-market capitalism, they must be informed. They must have an accurate and complete understanding of what they're paying for.

But how much of what American consumers now pay for product information really contributes to overall market efficiency? Not much. The vast majority of the money consumers are charged for the promotion of market efficiency really goes for the promotion of market inefficiency—helping one manufacturer to take sales away from other manufacturers with no resulting value creation.

Or, of course, the social engineering is designed to nudge us into buying a product or service that we ultimately don't need or that does not contribute to our overall well-being in the way the advertising implied. That fancy new car, for example, still only gets you from point A to point B, and your neighbors haven't really noticed the bigger, flashier, newer vehicle sitting in your driveway. They are far too consumed admiring their own new car.

Without such competition, of course, these same companies will argue, consumers would pay even higher prices, the quality of the product would be compromised, and there would be less choice. Competition is good for the consumer, they would argue. Fair enough, to a point. As an economy, however, we are so far beyond that point that it's no longer visible.

Thaler and Sunstein are right; we are constantly being nudged, and we are being nudged in ways we aren't consciously aware of but we are paying for. Both the government and the corporations who theoretically serve us are essentially exploiting us by preying on human psychology.

And the problem, of course, is getting worse now that we live and shop online. Advertising drives the Internet, reflecting early strategic decisions by the management of companies like Google that we were not aware of and had no vote in. According to *Business Insider*, advertisers spent more than $70 billion dollars online in 2016, surpassing for the first time the amount spent on TV ads.

As a result, the Internet is driven by clicks. While we think of the Internet in social and academic terms, like a cross between a huge library of knowledge and a global town hall meeting, it is, first and foremost, an advertising delivery system. Companies like Facebook are devoted, above all else, to getting you to spend more time on their site so that you will click on more ads.

But the Internet, we know, is a closed-loop system that reinforces existing opinions and patterns of behavior. It is no surprise, therefore, that Internet advertising is very concentrated, well beyond any level of concentration that Adam Smith would have felt acceptable for a free market. The ten leading ad-selling companies on the Internet account, in fact, for almost three-quarters of all advertising expenditures. And, no surprise, Facebook and Google receive the lion's share, and, more importantly, but not surprisingly, received 99 percent of the $13 billion *increase* in online advertising in 2016.

Once again, we must logically ask how much of the revenue growth realized by these two tech giants is a result of great performance and astute management and how much is due to the basic closed-loop structure of the Internet itself? Are the tech giants really that good, or just that lucky? Either way, it is society at large that has made their success possible. Ironic, to say the least, therefore, that society at large is the one getting fleeced for it.

What's worse is that we—the taxpayers, consumers, and residents—get fleeced on both sides of the sine wave. We get fleeced as the unintended consequences unfold, and we get fleeced when trends reach the tipping point and turn the other way, often with a big nudge that we ultimately pay for.

Let's look again at one of the government's more deliberate attempts at social engineering—home ownership. The first federal income tax was established in 1894, and it allowed for the deduction of all interest, including mortgage interest. The US Supreme Court, however, struck that law down, so in 1913, there was an amendment to the US Constitution. And it likewise allowed for the deduction of all interest expense.

The intent, however, probably had little to do with the promotion of home ownership since it was structured in such a way as to apply to only the top 1 percent of the population. And, in fact, the vast majority of homeowners did not have mortgages. At that time there was a cultural aversion to debt. Farmers were the one exception simply because managing a farm is very much like managing a business—you need working capital to run the business and make money.

In 1986, however, the government needed money and decided to sacrifice the consumer loan interest deduction to help raise it. By then, however, the desire to promote home ownership was well established, so the government eliminated all consumer loan interest other than the home mortgage deduction.

In December 2017, the federal government passed the biggest tax overhaul in thirty years that reduced or eliminated some of the tax incentives that historically nudged Americans in the direction of home ownership. By all accounts, however, this wasn't so much done in the interest of getting the government out of social engineering. Only the priorities have changed. The Trump administration apparently believes that giving American corporations and businesses a huge tax reduction will stimulate the economy. And although the administration appears to have no ideological commitment to balance the federal budget, it appears to have its limits, so it needed to find additional sources of revenue to offset the reduction in corporate tax assessments.

So it chose to reduce the social engineering emphasis on home ownership. The administration, of course, will argue it did no such thing since it simultaneously increased the standard deduction. But this is governance by obfuscation, which social engineering promotes in an effort to pursue social engineering that the voting public might not otherwise accept. In this case corporate America gets its tax cuts, because confusion has neutralized enough dissent to get the legislation through a Congress intent on nudging the economy through social engineering that favors business.

Whether that's good or bad for America's citizens and taxpayers only time will tell. Only one thing is certain. We are either reaching a peak tipping point favoring the country's business interests, or we are reaching a trough tipping point disfavoring the average worker and the environment. Eventually, one of those tipping points will be reached, and trends will turn back in the other direction.

The problem we face is that the sinusoidal cycles are getting longer and the amplitude—the height of the peaks and the depth of the troughs—are getting greater. And that is because of the increasing integration, greatly exaggerated and accelerated by technology, of our social, economic, and political systems.

The elimination of social engineering, unfortunately, is not an option, any more than the bicyclist can stand still without putting a foot down. Conservatives and progressives alike promote social engineering. They merely approach the topic from opposite directions.

This often gives the impression of irreconcilable differences. It certainly seems that way as we enter 2018. Republicans and Democrats seem incapable of working across the aisle. There is no common ground.

But if getting everyone into the same ideological camp is unlikely to happen, we can dampen the amplitude of the trends that social engineering, in the current environment, inevitably results in. We can accelerate the positive change we seek while acknowledging and diluting the negative impact of the negative change that is inherent to the closed-loop systems that dominate our economics, our society, and our politics.

We simply need to redirect the focus of our engineering away from the "I" and toward the "We." The differences in methodology preferred by progressives and conservatives are far less meaningful if the target of our engineering is the collective and inclusive "We" instead of the opportunistic and self-serving "I."

Consider, for example, the implication of such a simple change for one of the government's primary tools for social engineering today: the Internal Revenue Code. It is outrageously complicated not because of social engineering. It is outrageously complicated because of the overriding desire to engineer individual opportunities and behaviors. A loophole is not a loophole if it benefits everyone. A tax subsidy is not preferential if we all benefit.

A lot of the infighting over taxes simply goes away if we stop robbing Peter to pay Paul, as the saying goes. As would the overall complexity of the tax code. The costs of both enforcement and compliance would drop like a rock. And since both costs add zero value to the economy, we'd all benefit from the savings.

The state is a perpetual motion machine of unintended consequences. And because of both population growth and advancements in technology, the length and amplitude of the waves of change have dramatically increased. We're not going to change that any more than we can teach ourselves not to breathe.

What we can do, however, is ensure that our reaction to change is defined by the collective good rather than the individual opportunity. If the country is going to the dogs, let's empower the dogs that don't hunt. Let's empower the dogs that accept the inevitability of change, but who wish to nudge it in the direction of our collective well-being.

Summary

Change and social engineering are inevitable facts of life. However, we must channel them for the benefit of the collective "We," not the opportunistic "I."

- Corporate advertising that does not promote market efficiency from the consumer's perspective should be discouraged through media and tax regulations.
- Government attempts at social engineering should be minimized in deference to natural and democratically defined paradigms and shifts therein.
- The Internal Revenue Code should be greatly simplified, and individual loopholes should be eliminated.

CHAPTER 13

Democratic Elections

• • •

> The American Republic will endure until the day Congress discovers that it can bribe the public with the public's money.
>
> —Alexis de Tocqueville (1805–1859)

> It has been said that politics is the second oldest profession. I have learned that it bears a striking resemblance to the first.
>
> —Ronald Reagan (1911–2004)

WHILE MOST SCHOOLCHILDREN ARE TAUGHT that democracy first emerged in the Greek city-state of Athens around the fifth century BCE, there is little evidence that the concept was ever discovered at all. It is far more likely that a democratic variant of governance has existed since the first hunter-gatherers roamed the earth in self-identified clans or families.

Historians and political scientists have long been plagued by the imprecise nature of language and the almost infinite variations of governance that are both theoretically possible and actually exist, even today.

There are really two primary components of all governance. The first is power, and the second is obligation. Who has power, and how do they acquire it? And who are those in power obligated to govern for the benefit of?

Each component, of course, is part of a duality. And when it comes to the quality of governance, neither really matters in isolation. What matters is the degree of balance, or lack thereof, that exists between the two.

Power is the more straightforward of the two. Power belongs to whoever holds it, by definition. It can be acquired through war, heritage, or the popular vote. And, in the end, history has demonstrated that the path to power really doesn't matter all that much in terms of social and economic justice and advancement. Power is power.

Power, moreover, is fluid. It can appear to be stable for relatively long periods of time, but the only thing that can be said with certainly is that power always creates a challenge. It, too, is a duality. It, too, is defined by the balance, or imbalance, between those who hold power and those who want to take it away.

When it comes to governance, as a result, power is really the secondary consideration. How one comes to power is subordinate to how one uses that power. Democratically elected politicians, monarchs, and conquerors alike are capable of both good and bad governance. What matters most is who or what they feel an obligation to. On whose behalf do they exercise their power?

Obligation, however, is itself another duality. On the other side of leadership obligation is mutual obligation, or what might be more accurately described as deference. And, of course, deference is likewise a duality. I can defer to you because you have a gun to my head or because I, for whatever reason, choose to.

When these three elements of a nation or state—power, obligation, and deference—are in balance, there is peace and society has the best opportunity to progress, although there may be other influences as to how far it progresses and how quickly. When there is imbalance, however, progress stalls, and can, in fact, take a destructive turn.

If we define a society in terms of its common governance, we all want to belong to a society in which the three elements of power, obligation, and deference are in relative balance. We might say that the most balanced state allows the greatest amount of our social, political, and economic energy to be applied toward advancement.

When there is an imbalance, on the other hand, society does not progress because, as is true of all ecosystems in the universe, its energy is consumed with correcting the imbalance. As in the larger universe, balance is the ideal state toward which all energy is ultimately directed. Call it harmony if you like. It's all about inclusive stability in an advancing trajectory.

Of all the forms of governance that have existed over the course of history, it can be legitimately argued that American democracy has achieved the highest level of balance, which, in turn, allowed its social energy, shaped and directed by strong values of opportunity and achievement, to forge the American Century, from which the United States emerged as the lone superpower, the world's largest economy, and the primary architect of the digital world we now live in.

That is not to say that imbalance did not occur over the last two and a half centuries. Our social, political, and economic systems have become imbalanced on numerous occasions. In each case, however, our systems have shown a remarkable ability to self-correct and to reacquire something closer to equilibrium. In almost every case, however, while the most tragic consequences of imbalance have been avoided, the center of balance has nonetheless been moved from its original contextually defined position.

The slave trade that infected the American South in the early nineteenth century, for example, introduced largely for economic reasons, created an indefensible and unsustainable imbalance in the nation's social model. The Civil War ultimately eased the imbalance, but it clearly didn't abolish slavery per se. Racism was not eradicated and continues to absorb, even today, much of our social, economic, and political energy in nonproductive and destructive ways.

Technology, which has impacted the world in so many ways, has, more than anything else, empowered a heightened awareness of imbalances between power, obligation, and deference around the world. Women, the LGBTQ community, the physically and mentally challenged, the uneducated, and the poor, have always been enslaved, to varying degrees, by the white male oligopoly of the modern era.

Technology has both made the reality of this imbalance more transparent and raised the stakes. The white male oligopoly, if you will, has been able to lever its privilege to ever greater and greater advantage. The gap between the advantaged and the disadvantaged, as a result, has gotten much wider, and the impact of that gap far more meaningful.

Consider, for example, in a strictly material way, what it meant to be enslaved in ancient Egypt or the early nineteenth-century South. There were huge differences in the quality of life between the slaves and their masters, of course, but nobody had access to modern medicine, indoor plumbing, electricity, or efficient transportation. While the powerful lived in beautiful palaces and manor homes, the fundamental differences in the material quality of life were not as great as the difference between the world's poorest and most oppressed people today and their uberbillionaire fellow citizens.

This fundamental shift in degree and transparency has profound implications for governance in today's interconnected world. The more advanced an ecosystem is, the more it relies on balance, and the easier it is for that balance to be lost.

But if power and obligation are distinct facets of a governance ecosystem, they are interconnected. If a monarchy or religious state follows the principles of *noblesse oblige* first outlined by Homer, for example, it may further the collective good. Or, if such a sense of obligation is lacking, it may not.

A pluralistic democracy, of course, is designed to eliminate the need for self-imposed obligation. The electorate, through the power of the vote, can theoretically instill accountability and ensure that our leaders maintain an appropriate collective perspective and do not merely promote their own self-interests. (That's the theory, at least. The rise of the professional political class has obviously challenged that inherent accountability.)

In free-market capitalism, profits take the place of the voters. Profits, as Adam Smith described the capitalist economic system, are the invisible hand of democracy. Through the collective pursuit of unfettered self-interest, collective obligation is effectively realized.

Over time, as the shopkeeper and family farmer were replaced by the multinational corporation in the interest of scale and a further division of labor, however, the impartial governance of Smith's invisible hand of self-interest was forced to evolve. The lone shopkeeper's profits were relatively easy to measure. In the era of the large corporation, however, individual contributions are often organizationally removed from the discrete transactions of daily commerce.

This gave rise to a system of economic meritocracy. Individual executives are, in theory, granted power commensurate with their abilities. Power, in other words, is put in the hands of those most qualified to wield it effectively. Individual merit, in essence, becomes a proxy for profits.

Unfortunately, that is not the reality of corporate America today. The meritocracy has failed because merit has proven to be impossible to isolate and measure, particularly within an economic context that is changing daily. As I discussed in my previous book, *Understanding Business: The Logic of Balance*, the quest for corporate meritocracy, as a result, has effectively been hijacked by the executive and financial elite whose primary defining behavior has not been merit, but the promotion of their own self-interest.

Similar trends have unfolded in our political arena. Our democratic institutions have been hijacked by wealthy special interests that control the electoral levers. While money has always had influence in the democratic election process, we have moved beyond the tipping point of the electoral balance necessary for any degree of accountability. Political power, in essence, has been digitized. It is the ultimate manifestation of the either/or paradigm.

At best, such imbalance leads to stagnation as political divisions paralyze our political institutions. And at worst we have wasted energy and upheaval as one side seizes power and promotes its extreme partisan agenda only to be forced out of power by a disillusioned and angry electorate looking to upend the status quo. The sine waves of political reform become shorter, but more extreme, not unlike the storm patterns experienced as a result of climate change.

Part of the reason that American democracy has survived as long as it has, ironically, is the fact that it is not a pluralistic democracy to begin with. The Founding Fathers well understood the inherent risks of the democratic plurality and took great caution to minimize their impact. That is precisely why we have three branches of government, the electoral college, and major constitutional reforms require super-majorities at multiple levels of the electorate.

These political circuit breakers, such as they are, have, in fact, worked quite well in protecting the United States against pluralistic tyranny. What we have instead, unfortunately, is a two-headed Lernaean Hydra of polarization and stagnation. Virtually nothing happens in our state and national capitals except that the rich get richer and the poor and other marginalized groups are increasingly oppressed.

The explanation is not that our political circuit breakers have worked too well. The explanation is that, once again, the world has changed. An electoral democracy, even when circuit breakers are installed, simply won't achieve the balance necessary for social and economic progress in a world that is as crowded, small, and interconnected as ours currently is.

It is no coincidence that the democratic political model and the capitalist economic model are the cornerstones of American ideology. They share a common conceptual foundation. Both recognize the deductive correlation of cause and effect and utilize that universal and all-encompassing linkage to promote the collective good through individual rights, opportunities, and freedoms.

The resulting composite model of American governance worked rather well, in fact, in the agrarian, industrial, and postindustrial eras of the eighteenth, nineteenth, and twentieth centuries, when the population was growing, but still relatively small, technology had yet to wire us together twenty-four seven, and the social, political, and economic systems that collectively governed us were largely independent and self-contained.

None of those foundational elements, however, remains either independent or discretely manageable. We live in a more crowded world that has grown materially smaller and in which we are superficially interconnected around the clock and around the globe.

Unfortunately the carousel we find ourselves on continues to gain speed and momentum. It would be impractical, at best, to attempt to step off. Such a process is likely to lead to disaster as the people in power during the transition all jockey to position themselves at the most personally advantageous stepping-off point. In essence we would merely institutionalize the imbalance that currently plagues us.

We must, I believe, go back to the duality of power and obligation. As I've noted, power will always exist. It's as natural to our politics as oxygen is to the air we breathe. How it gets there is important, but far less important than what those in power do with that power. If those in power have the right sense of obligation, balance will be achieved, or nearly so, and incremental change in the machinery of allocating political power will be more practical for the simple reason that the need and the best path to satisfy that need will be much more obvious. As much as power enables obligation, obligation naturally defines the optimal mechanics for allocating power.

And what does that path look like?

For starters we must simply redefine the obligations of our political leaders. We must make them accountable not to their political base or wealthy supporters, but to the collective society at large. And while I am not so naïve as to suggest that saying it will make it happen, it won't happen until we articulate it. Perhaps an amendment to the US Constitution is warranted. I leave that to the scholars to decide. We must, however, articulate our collective belief that our collective well-being must trump our individual rights, liberties, and opportunities. We shouldn't deny people the opportunity to leverage their skills and hard work. But we should define that achievement in the context of the collective good.

Secondly, we must reduce political churn. Technology has ushered in the twenty-four seven news cycle and made virtually everyone a potential source of news. As a result, political elections cycles have been greatly compressed. Politicians are now in constant campaign mode. There is no time to do the hard work of governance when politicians are constantly focused on the next election.

This also creates a procedural disconnect similar to what we have experienced in the corporate sector. In this case we are electing not the most competent individuals with the highest integrity, but the best campaigners. And that means, more often than not, that we are allocating political power not to the most qualified, but to the most media savvy.

The problem is not the media. Of course the media is politically biased. It has always been biased. It is the very essence of humanity to have an opinion and a personal perspective. Objectivity, particularly in the political arena, simply does not exist.

The change that matters is not that the media has acquired bias, it is that the media cycle has been compressed down to the time it takes to tweet, and virtually everyone is a media contributor, few of whom feel any obligation to historically self-imposed standards of journalistic integrity. Clicks are all that matter.

We won't regulate our way out of the problem. That will only create unintended consequences that further aggravate the problem. We have to redefine the media ecosystem itself.

The place to start is the candid recognition of the impact of technology on the source and distribution of news and information. Contrary to what company executives have historically attempted to claim, Facebook, Google, and their tech colleagues are as much media companies as the *New York Times* and CNN. And they should be regulated accordingly.

Information is at the heart of every social, economic, and political system. It is the key to efficient markets, sound political policy, and a just society. While informational purity and integrity is an unattainable ideal, we must seek that standard. There is no viable or attractive alternative.

In the past we have largely regulated the media at its source through licensing of the airwaves that historically carried information and news. The Internet, however, has obliterated the relevance and effectiveness of that model.

In light of that current reality, we must regulate our political media not at its source, but at its destination. And while that may initially sound a lot like censorship, it doesn't have to be. Regulation doesn't have to be oppressive. It can be merely certified.

This topic, of course, could easily justify its own book, if not its own series. For our purposes here, let me merely suggest that we regulate our political information flow against the same model of power and obligation discussed in the beginning of the chapter. We don't regulate what the media says but why they say it. And we don't suppress any speech. We merely differentiate that which meets a predefined standard of promoting the collective good and that which is from a source that has not yet been vetted against that standard.

In the end, however, there will be hard limits to the degree that political information can be vetted and evaluated in terms of intent. Any attempt to define what is concurrently defines what isn't. And that's where loopholes and unintended consequences live.

Far better, I think, to recognize the inevitability of the pursuit of self-interest and simply change the structure of the game itself. In the case of politics, that means elongated election cycles.

If we elongate election terms, the risk of misinformation and political skullduggery is, by definition, reduced proportionately. While the negative impact of a bad electoral decision may be enhanced, the chances of that happening are greatly reduced by the simple fact that everyone, in the vernacular of Wall Street, has more skin in the game. This, in turn, will both enhance the effort and perspective that voters bring to the election, as well as the type of individual attracted to seek election in the first place. (It will also save the American taxpayer a whole lot of money.)

Such a fundamental change to the rules of the game, moreover, concedes the fact that as much as we should attempt to take the money out of politics, we are destined to fail. As history has demonstrated again and again, taking the money out of politics is akin to an eternal game of whack-a-mole.

If, however, we take the election out of the money, we minimize its corruptive influence. We fundamentally change, in fact, the very incentives that the moneyed elite have in choosing their candidate. It would be irrational to buy a car that is likely to last only a few years if it needs to last for a decade.

And that, in fact, is not a bad place to start. While there is no right or wrong number, what if we elected the president of the United States for a single ten-year term? The benefits, I believe, are self-evident in terms of cost, efficiency, continuity, and perspective.

As a practical matter, such a change would go a long way toward reducing the political distortion empowered by wealth, would allow our politicians to gain understanding and the efficiency and effectiveness that comes with experience without creating a permanent political class, and ensuring that we collectively elect politicians that are less partisan and that we can envision living with for a decade.

It's a place to start.

Summary

We must rethink our political governance and the information flows that drive it, with an emphasis on promoting the collective good and the promotion of inclusive, just advancement of the nation.

- Political news flows should be managed not at the source but at the destination. While we can't regulate truth, we can regulate purpose.

- We should make every effort to take the money out of politics, recognizing that, in the end, we will fail.
- We should minimize political churn by elongating all election cycles in the interest of cost, efficiency, effectiveness, and integrity.

CHAPTER 14

Centralization

• • •

The powers delegated by the proposed Constitution to the federal government are few and defined. Those which are to remain in the State governments are numerous and indefinite.

—James Madison (1751–1836)
Federalist Paper No. 45

One of the fundamental and far-reaching dualities of all governance systems is the trade-off between the local and the central. We are, in the most literal sense, the united states of America. We aren't the people who live between Mexico and Canada.

This, of course, is very much by design. While the Founding Fathers (some more than others) saw the need for a federal entity of governance, they took great pains to protect the autonomy of the thirteen original colonies. Essentially, they granted the federal government the right and responsibility to manage the country's defense, foreign diplomacy, and international commerce—the external stuff—while leaving all other areas of governance to the states and local communities.

While the federal government has greatly expanded these areas of influence over the years, the balance of power remains largely skewed, in breadth if not absolutely, in the direction of local control and influence. And, in fact, that made a lot of sense at the time.

For starters, the tools of governance at the time of the American Revolution, which primarily turn on the flow of information, were extremely limited in their reach and effectiveness over distance. Even the telegraph didn't come into existence until the 1830s. The telephone didn't come into wide use until the first years of the twentieth century. And the television didn't dominate our political news cycle until the 1950s.

Our personal and social identity was likewise largely localized. While ethnic and cultural identity was obviously important, most of us identified most closely with our families, which were largely stable and geographically localized.

For the last two centuries, of course, all of that has changed. Technology has given us personal mobility, pushed the cost of communication to near zero, and extended the reach of that communication across borders and time zones. We are, in the most fundamental sense, a wired, integrated nation today.

Our governance, however, does not mirror this sea change. While the federal government has expanded its power in new ways, much to the chagrin of many state and local politicians, the structure of power has not been fundamentally redefined. From issuing driver's licenses to managing health care, the American social and economic systems are still largely governed at the local level.

Globally, there has actually been some migration back to localized governance and identity. With the breakup of the Soviet Union and the dismantling of the former European empires, the number of independent nations has grown dramatically. At its founding in 1945, the United Nations had only fifty-five member nations. Today, there are close to two hundred.

The role of technology in shifting the collective/local governance paradigm has been profoundly bidirectional. On the one hand, technology has obliterated geographic borders in terms of the effectiveness and efficiency of governance. This same centralization and consolidation, however, has compromised the basic human need and desire for personal identity, often encouraging people to seek a stronger local identity to help offset the homogenizing impact of that same technology.

A lot of the localization of governance, moreover, reflects the difficulty that all systems of governance have historically had with protecting the rights and culture of minority groups. The breakup of the European colonies and the Soviet Union were driven, in part, by this common governance shortcoming. And we still see forces acting in that direction in places like Spain and Russia, where minority groups have long sought independence and autonomy.

The record of the United States in terms of protecting minority rights is not materially better than the rest of the world. We did, after all, tolerate slavery for more than two hundred years before Lincoln issued the Emancipation Proclamation, and it would still take another century before African Americans were given the effective power of the vote in all US states. (Even that is being generous, perhaps.) Women did not get the vote for almost 150 years after the Founding Fathers declared, "We the people," and launched a government devoted to "liberty and justice for all."

It would not be until 1950, in fact, that the vote was granted to all white men. Before that time, many states used property and employment requirements to restrict the power of governance to privileged white males.

But do the exceptions really justify a new rule? Should we merely accept that no form of governance adequately protects the rights of minorities, however defined, and fragment our governance accordingly? Or do we want to solve the problem?

Was it really the best course of action to protect "Southern" culture in the Reconstruction South? Does it really make sense in terms of gender equality to protect the Puritanical vestiges of colonial New England? Is the Western gunslinger and the self-indulgent cattle rancher who laid unfounded claim to the wide-open ranges of the American West really the model we want to enshrine and perpetuate there?

What, exactly, are we trying to protect?

I am as much a part of history as anyone. I honor our collective and individual culture. But that doesn't mean I must accept every moral judgment ever made or cultural attribute ever adhered to. People make mistakes. People learn and grow. Protecting the past can't, or shouldn't, stop us from moving on.

There are, nonetheless, many aspects of culture that must be preserved. Forced cultural assimilation is not the answer. We are, as a nation, enriched by our cultural diversity.

And, of course, religious freedom is a defining, foundational aspect of American exceptionalism. Without it we are not Americans. Do we really want, therefore, to allow all the Islamophobes, for example, to move to one state with the intent of creating an anti-caliphate state? (That is obviously a rhetorical question.)

Localization versus federalism is not an either/or choice any more than nationalism versus globalism is. Common governance does not have to mean homogenization. If anything, I think, by forcing ourselves to accommodate diversity, we empower our individual identity.

Culture and ethnic localities are not always good. Do we really want to preserve racial slums or poor, crime-ridden ethnic neighborhoods? Neither poverty nor crime, much less drug addiction, are cultural identities.

Localization, like everything else in the universe, is part of a duality. It has both pro and con facets. And that ledger is defined, in large part, by a larger context of reality that is, as I have maintained throughout this book, changing dramatically. When it comes to localization, in fact, the pro side of the ledger is increasingly barren. If oppression is the other side of the coin of entitlement and preservation of the historical status quo, that coin has flipped.

For starters, the cost of governance has skyrocketed. This is, in part, merely a reflection of the rise in wages. The bigger impact, however, has come from the exponential increase in the number and breadth of government services provided and necessitated by the modern world.

The Department of Motor Vehicles, for example, didn't exist a century ago. There were no labor or environmental boards. There was no Medicare or Medicaid. And the states made no effort to license professionals from engineers to barbers. All told, governance was narrowly defined and relatively inexpensive to provide.

Today, however, nearly one in five American workers are employed by the government at the federal, state, or local level. Nearly half of all union members work for the government. And public-sector employees belong to a union at more than five times the rate of workers in the private sector.

Collectively, the fifty states now spend almost $2 trillion per year, ranging from a low of $3,800 per person in Florida to a high of $14,000 per person in Alaska. The two most populous states, California and Texas, spend $6,800 and $4,600 *per person*, respectively.

There is little question, of course, that given current technology, virtually all the services managed by the states could be managed more efficiently at the federal level. The cost of the local administration of government services, however, is only the tip of the iceberg of the true cost of local governance. The biggest impact occurs in its effectiveness and potential impact.

Many large federal government programs, like Medicare and Medicaid, are governed at the state level but funded by the federal government. That means we have two levels of governance, which means, in the vernacular of business, we have double the overhead expense. Do we really gain anything by passing those taxpayer funds through two government bureaucracies instead of one?

Think of the amount of money, moreover, that businesses that exist in more than one state spend each year simply trying to understand the impact of local regulations and state laws. Or the practical and real financial cost to a job seeker who moves across state lines in search of employment. All of which is above and beyond the very real cost of the forfeited scale and its impact on purchasing costs and structural governance costs.

One of Adam Smith's most fundamental assumptions was the existence of free and efficient markets. Which has been, indirectly, the entire justification for commercial globalization. But why do we worry about trade with Mexico and ignore the barriers that hinder trade between California and Wyoming, for example?

And what about law enforcement? The 2012 Bureau of Justice Statistics Census of State and Local Law Enforcement Agencies found that there were close to eighteen thousand distinct state and local law enforcement agencies operating in the United States at that time. What a great time to be a criminal. And what a terrible time to be a taxpayer.

Does anyone really believe that having almost four times more law enforcement agencies than hospitals (5,564) or educational institutions of higher learning (4,627) is more effective or cost efficient than an expanded FBI, ATF, or ICE? While there is still a lot of local crime to be solved, the most egregious crimes are not confined geographically. And just as soon as a criminal crosses some artificial boundary separating those eighteen thousand distinct agencies, the cost of catching that criminal goes up and the chances of catching him or her goes down.

This has nothing to do with having police officers that live in and understand the local community. That's a function of residence, not governance. And remember the existence of universal duality. When we empower a local law enforcement agency to localize its law enforcement tactics, we are authorizing it to localize its law enforcement tactics. For every empathetic rural sheriff, there will be some suburban agency that arms itself to the teeth and utilizes enforcement tactics much like the military would use were it invading a hostile nation.

The pro and con of local governance is the inevitable and universal duality of all things. On the one hand, it accommodates local adaptation. On the other, such adaptation effectively impedes collective progress on any number of social and economic fronts.

Nowhere has this duality been more pronounced than in the area of education. While the federal government has increasingly inserted itself into the education process, beginning with President George W. Bush's No Child Left Behind Act, and expanding with President Barack Obama's Every Student Succeeds Act, our schools remain largely locally governed.

Which is precisely why many public high schools have implemented ridiculous dress codes that result in far more confusion than decency. And why one elderly woman in the small town where I myself went to high school could tie up the local school board's time and attention because she thought the school's sports nickname—the Red Devils—promoted devil worship among the youth of the community.

The most obvious distortion this creates is the extreme inequity in services and quality that exists between wealthy and poor school districts. We think of this as somehow just and the logical consequence of our cultural commitment to rugged individualism. But is it?

Doesn't the cost of supporting the wealthier districts drive up housing costs for everyone? And while that clearly reinforces and expands social inequity, don't the wealthy suffer as well? What happens, as had already happened in exclusive enclaves like Aspen, Colorado, when the people who the wealthy rely on for the provision of goods and services can no longer afford to live in the area where those services are in demand?

And can the hedge fund manager from Westchester really prosper if the companies he or she invests in can't find qualified workers to staff their operations or have seen the market for the middle class version of their products or services evaporate?

What happens when the disenfranchised among us attain critical mass and take control of the electoral process, as is their clearly defined right, and throw all of the bastards out? (We already know the answer, of course.) Is that really progress? Is that really creating a land of individual opportunity?

There clearly comes a tipping point, and we have long since passed it by, when the promotion of individual opportunity and individual rights and freedoms is so effective that it becomes self-defeating. I refer to it as the sine-wave theory of the universe. Because everything is part of a duality, every trend is ultimately self-correcting. Every trend, no matter how attractive or unattractive it may be, must and will come to an end. However you believe we got here, this is where we are.

The law of large numbers was first proved by Swiss mathematician Jacob Bernoulli (1654–1705). It holds that reality gets closer and closer to theoretical probabilities as the number of instances increases. Flip a coin enough times and you are sure to get results that verify the fifty-fifty probability of getting heads or tails.

But it also applies to governance. Yes, centralization will inevitably lead to some homogenization. But that isn't always a bad thing. It also means that some of the extremes are tempered. It may mean, for example, that criminals can't drive to Arizona, Mississippi, or Louisiana, the three states with the least restrictive gun laws, according to the Law Center to Prevent Gun Violence, to buy the weapons they need to commit violent crimes in the more populated states like Texas or California. Young adults in Kansas and Nebraska, likewise, cannot effectively drive across the border to Colorado to purchase marijuana until their own states vote to legalize it.

Whatever your position on either of these issues, and I am in favor of decriminalizing marijuana and other recreational drugs, do we really want to govern these issues on a patchwork, state-by-state basis? How is that protecting anything of consequence? (In fact, it is just creating confusion, as we are now discovering in the battle over the regulation of marijuana between the states and US attorney general.)

Will the two coasts wipe out the cultural identity of the Midwest, which many elites in those states derisively refer to as the "flyover states," if we federalize more of our governance? Some may want to. But even with centralized governance, what are they going to do? Culture and governance, in the end, have limited crossover.

My wife is Chinese. And, of course, China has a completely different system of governance than the United States. That distinction, however, has no impact whatsoever on her ability to celebrate and embrace Chinese culture. And for the nine years that I lived in China working for a US multinational company, the reverse was true as well. There was nothing about living there that prevented me from being an American, however I chose to define what that meant. Sure, I couldn't vote, but in every way that I considered central to my identity and culture, I lived pretty much as I did in New York, where I was born.

In a variation of Bernoulli's law of large numbers, localization actually harms residents of the less populous states in many important areas. Health insurance is one of them.

President Obama astutely recognized that insurance is a numbers game. The very concept of insurance is to spread risk over as a large a population as possible. The better for everyone. And President Obama did just that with the Obamacare mandate, which has now been rescinded by the Republican administration in the theoretical interest of economic individualism.

It is, however, a political ruse. Americans are already required to buy insurance they may not individually want when they purchase a car or borrow money from the bank to purchase a home. The elimination of the mandate will inevitably drive up the cost of health insurance for those who need it most, regardless of their ability to pay.

And, of course, nothing exists in isolation. A healthy person may not need health insurance today, but if they get sick or injured, they will need health care. And US hospitals are required, by law, to provide it, regardless of the patient's ability to pay. The practical result of the elimination of the health insurance mandate, in other words, is not that the healthy among us no longer have to subsidize the ill and elderly, it is that the ill and elderly will have to subsidize the currently healthy who fall ill. Is that really justice, as the Republicans have claimed?

On another front, fully 64 percent of Fortune 500 companies are currently incorporated in the state of Delaware, a state with only 0.30 percent of the United States population, or less than one million residents. And few of those companies even have an office there.

This is not a function of Delaware's longevity as one of the original thirteen colonies or its strategic position on the map. Google, Facebook, Amazon, and Yelp are all incorporated there. And the reason is simple. Delaware has the most business-friendly legal statutes and a governance model designed to service corporate needs.

That's great for the Fortune 500, and for the people of Delaware, but is it great for America? Under any circumstances, is it really just that less than one in 315 Americans gets to decide how corporations are to be governed?

Amazon has decided to build a second headquarters and is promising to spend $5 billion and to create up to fifty thousand new jobs. The company has put the location up for bids and local governments are lining up to give away millions, if not billions, in tax subsidies and infrastructure improvements.

It's all perfectly legal. We've actually incentivized Amazon to do it. And some lucky locality will benefit, although the return on investment for local taxpayers is often questionable in such bidding wars. But will the American economy really benefit? And can whatever local economy that is chosen really prosper long term without the rest of the country prospering as well?

Is local governance really preserving the regional and cultural identity we want to preserve? Or are we spending an awful lot of money in governance bureaucracy costs and aggravating unproductive competition between the states, and actually undermining our collective progress?

The fact is that local identity is already protected by the very structure of our federal government. We have three largely equal branches of government, and one of those branches, the powerful legislative branch, has allocated significant power to one chamber, the US Senate, that literally defies proportional representation. Every state, regardless of population or strategic or economic importance, has two equally empowered US senators.

In fact, even that is not entirely true. The smaller states actually have more senatorial power than the more populated states because much of the work of the US Senate is performed by committees, and the leadership positions on those committees is assigned by seniority. And, not surprisingly, it is the smaller states that tend to have the most senior US senators because of a variation of Bernoulli's law. It is the less populous states that are more likely to have an ongoing imbalance in power between the two political parties.

The Appropriations, Armed Services, Commerce, Finance, and Foreign Relations committees of the US Senate are commonly considered to be that governing body's most powerful committees. The current chairmen of those five committees, all Republicans, however, have been elected by voters who collectively represent only 7 percent of the US population. The current ranking members of those same committees, all Democrats, were elected by voters who collectively represent 10 percent of the US population, but if you take out Bill Nelson (D-FL), the ranking member of the Commerce, Science, and Transportation Committee, the remaining four were elected by less than 4 percent of the US electorate.

There is, in other words, virtually no chance that the less populous states are going to be oppressed by the more populous states. There are plenty of checks and balances already in place to prevent it.

Summary

We must reassess the allocation of governance responsibility and power between the states and the localities and the federal government in the interests of cost effectiveness, overall efficiency, and justice. Specifically, we should quickly centralize responsibility for the following:

- Education
- Law enforcement
- Commerce
- Environmental management
- Medicine and insurance
- Vehicle and driver management

Moving Forward
...

Conclusion

• • •

*If you do not change direction, you may
end up where you are heading.*

—Laoxi (Lao Tzu) (604 BCE–531 BCE)

As I wrote in the opening paragraph, the premise of this book is pretty simple. Or at least straightforward. It is that the economic, political, and social systems and institutions that collectively define the United States and shape the lives of Americans have become both more complex and more integrated over time. We have, as a result, surpassed the tipping point at which the supremacy of the individual, the "I" in all of our freedoms and liberties, threatens the hope and vitality that gave life and purpose to American exceptionalism and the American Century.

I recently read a delightful history, *Moral Combat: How Sex Divided American Christians & Fractured American Politics*, by historian R. Marie Griffith. She is the John C. Danforth Distinguished Professor in the Humanities at Washington University in Saint Louis, and the book chronicles the history of our very vocal and divisive social and political debate over issues of sex in the United

States. I will spare you the details, but consider that less than one hundred years ago, we were actively debating whether sexual intercourse between a married man and woman not specifically attempting to procreate was immoral.

At about that same time, the C. G. Johnson company invented the electric garage door opener, which I have long considered to be one of the great wonders of modern technological convenience, having lived in northern climates all my life. And, of course, then came the torrent of all things digital, including the Internet, in the closing decades of the twentieth century.

Again, I won't bore you with all of the technological change that has occurred in my own lifetime. It will just make me sound old. But consider this: I was well into my corporate business career, running a major division of a US multinational company, when PowerPoint was created by Robert Gaskins and Dennis Austin at a software company named Forethought, Inc. in 1987. It originally ran only on Apple Macintosh computers, if you can believe it, and I'm sure both Gaskins and Austin have since changed their names and gone into hiding.

In all seriousness, however, the change has been swift and all-encompassing. Technology has transformed every aspect of how we live, learn, work, and play. From cradle to grave, our lives have been digitized. Everything has changed.

Yet, at a different level, nothing has changed. Philosophically, we continue to struggle with the same questions. Our needs haven't changed. Our desires haven't changed. Abraham Maslow's hierarchy of needs is as valid today as it was in 1943, when he introduced it. And it was as relevant then as it was one thousand years before that.

I believe, in fact, that technology doesn't change anything. It merely reveals the reality that is already there. Technology is, in the end, transparency. Every advance in technology merely serves to peel back another layer of the onion.

Of course it changes what we do and how we do it. But in the immortal words of Vinnie Antonelli in the 1990 classic *My Blue Heaven*, "the truth is still the truth." That never changes. It seems to, mind you. But that's because we sometimes ask the wrong question.

The jury is still very much out as to whether or not technology, as we now apply it, will ultimately prove to be a net positive or not. I personally believe that we will ultimately have to find a way to unplug once in a while. We will have to manage our technology and not let it manage us to the extent it does today.

We must ultimately redefine the workplace as well. I don't know where we will work or with what tasks we will occupy our workdays. I do know, however, that we must recognize that no organization can succeed without trust. We must recognize that life and business cannot always be reduced to a spreadsheet or a financial model. We must recognize that the division of labor has run its course and that commerce and commercial creation is best approached holistically and collaboratively. Progress is incremental, but creation is inspired, and inspiration is not one-dimensional. It is cultivated, not made.

Social media, in its current form, will go the way of AOL. We will see the digital community for what it is, a digital cigarette. Just as we ultimately came to recognize that the cigarette is nothing more than a nicotine delivery system, we will come to recognize that social media is little more than a platform for self-absorption and the addiction to potential celebrity that never comes.

In the end, talking is a vastly overrated form of communication and connection. Actual behavior, particularly in the context of physical presence, including touch, is far more important. If a picture is worth a thousand spoken words, an action is worth ten thousand pictures. The human bond is not one that can be sustained at the deepest level over the digital airwaves.

We all want to be loved, but we don't want to be loved as performers, which is precisely why so many celebrities feel isolated and alone despite the adoring crowds. Performance can be art. It can't be life.

Our children will tire of pretending, and pretending to pretend, and pretending to pretend they're pretending. Because pretension may inspire change, but it doesn't create change in any direct way.

Who we are hasn't really changed. There is no Generation X. There are no millennials or baby boomers. There are people who behave like they belong to these generations just as there are people who behave like they live in California or New York or Chicago. But we're all really the same in the ways that matter most.

Because if there is any one truth that all of this technology has revealed beyond a shadow of a doubt, it is the simple truth that we are all in this together. We are, to put it more precisely, in "IT" together. The places and the things and the people we share and project are all just facets of the same reality. I am the sun and the stars. The sun and the stars are the energy that powers it all. And that energy is me. Not six of one, half dozen of the other. Just one. And the one is many. Me, myself, and I really are we, ourselves, and us—and, in fact, it, that, and those.

Einstein is reported to have said, "Doing the same thing repeatedly and expecting different results is the definition of insanity." He wasn't wrong. He was Einstein. But we missed the point nonetheless.

The Native Americans had it right. You can't stick your toe in the same river twice. The mere facts of history have little to teach us because history unfolds in a unique labyrinth of context that exists in a nearly infinite number of dimensions all at the same time. (Understanding that context is where the historian comes in.)

Time, in the end, is simply the natural beat of reality revealing itself. We control the speed of the revelation, which is why technology appears to accelerate time. The beat of time, however, is an arbitrary convention, just like the clock and the calendar. The future, I believe, already exists, albeit in infinite variations, and always has. And it will reveal itself at whatever pace we are prepared to accept it.

What it will reveal and what it all means I don't pretend to know. And I'm not sure I care. I don't want to miss the journey.

What I do know is that we—Americans, the human race, however you want to define "us"—are raising a lot of dust. We're making a lot of noise. And while I never did understand my daughters' cries in the middle of the night when they were newborns, I knew they wanted something to change. Start with the diaper, move on to the bottle, and keep plodding ahead from there.

The collective cries of Americans today are deafening. We're disillusioned. We're worried. We're lonely. It's not working out the way we hoped it would. It's not working out the way the people we trusted told us it would. It's just not working out. As comfortable as our lives have become, we don't feel the sense of justice and security we have to feel before we can attack connection, self-respect, and self-actualization. We're stuck on the first two rungs of Maslow's ladder.

If there is one thing I've learned in all of my contemplation, it is that when something feels wrong, don't look for the reason. Look for the imbalance. Something may be happening. Or it may not. Either way, there is an imbalance somewhere, and it is the imbalance, not the forces creating it, that is at the heart of all our fear and anxiety.

The American experiment, as de Tocqueville referred to it, has been a smashing success. To think that a single governance system has lasted, with a few tweaks along the way, for almost 250 years and has produced what is no less than American exceptionalism is beyond remarkable.

But there is an imbalance. There is a misalignment between the economic, social, and political systems that I have collectively called governance. As our population has grown and our technology has expanded, we have accelerated the pace at which we live, work, and play. And in so doing, an imbalance that has probably been there all along has revealed itself, just like the washing machine that starts knocking when it goes into its spin cycle.

So, what do we do?

There was a time that we could, as our ancestors did, build a new washing machine. It's theoretically possible but comes at huge risk. They did it at a time when the most advanced weapon on the planet could shoot about three rounds per minute, was accurate at a maximum distance of about twenty yards, and fired a little round ball that could kill you but wouldn't explode inside of you. It's another duality. Along with Facebook and Google, technology has given us weapons of mass destruction that could obliterate us all in a heartbeat.

I've also found that when you unleash the chain reaction of change, you can never be really sure of where it will lead. It's the law of unintended consequences, which technology has greatly amplified. I've developed a fondness, as a result, for tweaking rather than tearing down. And if my four-plus decades in business has taught me anything, it is that change is good, but never change what you don't understand until you do. And when you first think that you understand something, chances are good that you don't.

Our social, political, and economic institutions have evolved over a very long period of time. And I don't see any reason why we have to throw them out or start over. Remember, reality hasn't really changed; it has only been further revealed.

The good news is that by simply changing our perspective, the changes we need to make will become obvious to all of us. As Dr. Wayne Dyer (1940–2015), the author of *Your Erroneous Zones* (1976), one of the best-selling books of all time, wrote, "If you change the way you look at things, the things you look at change." Or, as one of the great comic minds of all time, Robin Williams (1951–2014), put it, "No matter what people tell you, words and ideas can change the world."

We don't have to repudiate the "I" in American. We just have to put the "I" in the right context. We have to recognize that "I" is just one facet of "We." It's always been that way, of course, but it mattered less in an analog world in which the fabric of our social, economic, and political systems was less tightly woven.

I won't even attempt to define the detailed path we should follow. As is appropriate in the integrated world that technology has now revealed, that should be a collaborative effort. We'll need role players, impact players, functional experts, and a whole bunch of people to cheer them on and keep them motivated. I am convinced, however, that once we start to think and act collectively, the road forward to a more prosperous and just America will become obvious.

There are, nonetheless, a few steps that I believe will be helpful, if not absolutely necessary. Each can be accomplished in a very short period of time without a lot of effort. And while critics will be quick to point out that there will be some expense involved, all can be revenue neutral if we approach the change holistically.

These steps include:

1. **Extend Medicare to all.**
   It's obviously not a perfect system. But it exists and has withstood the test of time. The overriding need is to take financial health risk off the table so that we can all focus our efforts and our thoughts toward collective justice and economic prosperity. This move alone will take tremendous amounts of non-value-added cost out of the healthcare system. And

it will give us consistency and continuity. People will not be penalized or rewarded for the state they choose to live in.
2. **Implement a universal wage.**
This is not a new idea. Many progressive Enlightenment thinkers advocated it for the same reasons it is so necessary today. Technology and development have eliminated the natural safety net historically provided by our natural environment. People can no longer live without income. To deprive every human being a basic sustainable income is both immoral and impractical. If we want people to embrace technology, and there is little question that it is the surest path to collective progress, we have to eliminate the many current reasons to fear it.
3. **Make higher education available to all at no cost.**
This is a variation of the universal wage. If we want people to contribute to collective prosperity and not just feed off of it, we must give them the tools to do so. That doesn't mean, however, we should limit education to the STEM subjects. Technology can teach us about itself. It is a task to which its pattern recognition is ideally suited. What we must teach one another is how to think creatively, how to collaborate, and how to empathize and tolerate.
4. **Elongate election cycles.**
We will never take the money out of elections. We must take the elections away from the money. Elongated election cycles will help to offset the acceleration of time that technology has brought with it and are a practical recognition of the complexity and pace of the world today. For starters, let's limit the US presidency to one ten-year term, and let's limit the terms of US senators and representatives to two ten-year terms, and unlimited five-year terms, respectively.

5. **Channel and regulate the public flow of information.**
   We must end the charade that Facebook and Google and the other tech giants are unbiased platforms merely facilitating the flow of information. Not all information is the same. And when it comes to news, you can't report the news without creating the news. If Facebook wants to be a social media company, force it to get out of the news business. And while the truth cannot be regulated, we can rate it and certify it, just as we do with many other products. We shouldn't censor the news, perhaps, but we should channel it and certify its providers in much the same way we have historically regulated all media companies.

This is not meant to be an exhaustive list. It is merely a place to start. And I have intentionally left many of the details open to discussion, both to allow for collaboration and to allow for an incremental approach to change, the pace of which we can control based on our collective appetite and the results realized along the way.

At the same time, we must more adequately regulate executive and investor compensation. We must redefine corporate purpose to include collective justice and prosperity and give employees a legitimate stake in corporate decision-making. We must put hard limits on corporate advertising and marketing and demand enhanced accountability for the environment, which itself will temper the forces of globalization.

We must stop commercializing society, including social and personal justice, and recognize our common humanity and collective rights and freedoms. That includes universal access to the levers of legal justice and a new approach to criminal justice that is less self-reinforcing, puts more emphasis on prevention, and is more just.

We must stop trying to regulate human behavior through the criminalization of recreational drug use and sexual morality, with obvious exceptions for any behavior that is abusive or directly impacts the rights, freedoms, and dignity of others.

We must eventually rewrite the Internal Revenue Code to remove all attempts at social and economic engineering. The tax code should be simple and neutral. Any attempts at social engineering, and some are justified, should be transparent and proactive and don't belong in the tax code, where they are often hidden and their impact and return are difficult to isolate and measure.

None of this will be easy. The people who have the power to change have the least incentive to promote it. They will fight to protect the status quo that has benefited them so well.

They will use the language of rationalization to resist, just as they have used such language to get what they have today. We must resist. Let us recognize that language is an arbitrary human convention that is imprecise at best and misleading or false when abused.

Let us think with our hearts as well our heads. We know what's right. We know what is just. We know progress when we see it. Let us have strength in our knowing.

The world hasn't changed so much as it has further revealed itself. We shouldn't reject either the truth that has been revealed or the technology that has brought it into our collective consciousness. We should seek more, not less.

In the end we should not subvert or discourage the individual self. We simply need to recognize that it exists within a larger context. It exists within a reality in which all things are interconnected and interdependent. In accepting that truth, we don't reject the past. We empower the future. We set the stage for a more just and prosperous world for we, ourselves, and us.

From the Author

• • •

Thank you for taking the time to read this book. I hope it has made you think in a slightly different way about our country and our society.

If it did, I humbly ask that you leave a review on Amazon and Goodreads, and any other book review site you use. I also hope you will send a quick note to friends and family on Twitter, Facebook, or any other form of social media.

As an indie author I rely almost completely on word of mouth for my book sales. What will only take a couple of minutes for you will make a world of difference for me. And isn't that the best kind of "we"?

About the Author

• • •

Gary Moreau is a retired corporate executive who made his career in economics, business consulting, executive coaching, and speaking services. He has studied economic systems in the United States, China, and Europe. His firsthand knowledge and experience led to *We, Ourselves, and Us*, his latest political and economic treatise.

Moreau was named by the World Economic Forum as one of its Global Leaders for Tomorrow in 1993. He has also been honored by the Conference Board for his work in organizational performance and corporate governance.

From his home in the Midwest, Moreau has authored nine books, including two fictional novels under the pseudonym Avam Hale. For more information about his work, he invites you to e-mail him at gary@gmoreau.com and follow him on Twitter @gmoreaubooks.

www.ingramcontent.com/pod-product-compliance
Lightning Source LLC
Chambersburg PA
CBHW020653220526
45464CB00001B/414